Wicca Altar

The Ultimate Guide to Approach Wiccan Moon Magic, Crystal and Candle Magic

ISABEL SCOTT

PUBLISHED BY: Green Book Publishing LTD

58 Warwick Road

London W5 5PX

Legal & Disclaimer

The information contained in this book and its contents is not designed to replace or take the place of any form of medical or professional advice; and is not meant to replace the need for independent medical, financial, legal or other professional advice or services, as may be required. The content

Table of Contents

Part 1: Introduction

Before we get started, I would like to thank and congratulate you for downloading your copy of Wicca Altar: The Ultimate Guide to Approach Wiccan Moon Magic, Crystals and Candle Magic. Whether you're just exploring your curiosity about this fairly unusual religion, or whether you've decided you're definitely ready to wade further into the waters of Wiccan wisdom, you'll find solid information and practical advice in these pages. Before we get started. With this comprehensive guide to the tools used in Wiccan practice, you have taken the first steps towards understanding the power of magick and incorporating it into your daily life. In this brief but detailed book, you'll get to learn about everything you could possibly need to add in your bag of knowledge about the tools that are used in a spellwork, that includes how to choose, do the cleansing, and consecrate tools you use to perform magickal work. You'll also learn about altar setup and how to adorn your altar appropriately for each sabbat. As a special bonus, an in-depth look at divination tools and their uses is also included.

The altar and tools provide the basis of every magickal practice and spellwork, which means that an in-depth understanding of their uses and maintenance is fundamental to a successful relationship with the craft. By the time you finish reading this book, you will have all the knowledge of Wiccan tools and altar setup you need to bring great magick into your life. Be blessed.

Chapter 1: Origins of the Wiccan Altar

The altar is a raised object on which a Wiccan places ritual tools and offerings to the gods and goddesses above.

These offerings were generally burnt food, or coins or herbs. In true Wiccan culture, sacrifices are banned. Even if the Pagan were not worshiping Satan, he/she would still kill animals for spells.

With that in mind, the Christian altar is not as clean as it may seem today. However, the cleanliness that we see in Christian altars today influenced Wiccan altars as we know them. The Pagan Altar idea of keeping all one's tools used for the spell on the altar so as to keep them sacred is also integrated into the Wiccan altar. The Wiccan altar is very important in traditional rituals, so if a spell calls for an altar, you should use one (even if it is just a table or mound of earth with a cloth) so that you can say a consecration prayer over it. There are so many ways you can use an altar; often you do not have to build one yourself if you have ANYTHING that can keep your tools off the unconsecrated ground.

Chapter 2: Types of Altar

There are various types or kind of altars that Wiccans might choose to go with or use to carry out a ritual. The material Wiccans use in their altars may vary depending on the kind of rite they want to perform. You find that some belief that wood from maple tree is the only one allowed while others say wood from an oak tree is actually the best. You find that many circles have different types of wood which are believed to bring out or result to giving good magic qualities. Let us look at an example in a Wiccan tradition oak is seen as a symbol believed to greatly strengthen the rite being performed. And in another tradition maple is seen as the strongest. It is up you as an individual to choose what to use, either a tree stump or a coffee table it narrows down to your preference. You might want to locate your altar away from areas that have high traffic like hallways. Let us go through some of the different types of altars found in a Wiccan house hold.

House altar: This altar arrangement is best stationed in a more central part in your the house, for instance one might choose for example your living room and set it up on top of a sideboard. Not much changes with this type of altar but same time is adjust with the change in times. The family is at liberty to decorate the altar and be there to admire and enjoy the changing appearance throughout the changing seasons. Non-pagans do create their altar without really see it as an altar but just a home decoration.

Personal altar: It remains permanently stationed in one place of an individual liking (a Wiccan) and on display, you should be the only person seeing it. One might choose to place in their closet or even in their bedroom. There are other more places of one's choice to place your personal altar such as a shelf or a windowsill. You might want it to place it on your bedside table where you can place the statuettes of the gods and even goddess.

You will find that many non-pagans do create such type of altar although the non-pagans would not consider calling it altar. Also some might put on display items that draw significance from the religion they identify with such as sacred literature.

Working altar: The working altar is so different from personal altar and house altar since this type of altar should not be put on display. Remember it's important to note that at the beginning and after finishing ritual and spell is performed, you must cleanse it. It is best done in a working space that can be easily stripped bare to fit your different desires as you set up for another ritual or spell. Small table might be used by a coven. Perhaps you might choose a square piece of scarf or a smooth piece of wood to function as an altar top, mostly oi would be something you can just fold after you rituals practice.

Chapter3: Altar Items

The pentacle is often carved into magical tools to give them the proper energy so that the tools do not need to seek energy from undesirable entities.

There are so many options for wearing the pentacle that it is not funny. You can even have it printed on shoes. If you have the pentacle printed on your shoes and sewn into your robe, you do not need jewelry covered in pentacles. You can save the jewelry for gemstones that will help the ritual spell of the night you are celebrating.

Broom

The broom is a symbol of strength in the Wiccan religion. Contrary to media portrayal, it is not something you can fly on. The broom is merely a decorative item, but sometimes you need it to "sweep" negative energy – or other magical energies you do not want interfering with your magic – out of your spell.

A witch's broom is wooden and has straw at its head. You do not want to use a store-bought broom, as it will not have any magical energy due to it's being processed. You will want to make your own or if you must buy one, get one from a Wiccan supply store, as their brooms are handmade and will have the energy you need.

If you decide to make your own, be sure that you sand down the handle because splinters are not a fun thing to deal with and you do not want to have any distractions when you are performing a spell. Splinters can prove to be a very big distraction, one that can throw off the balance of your magic.

Athame

The athame is a ritual dagger, traditionally double-edged, that serves as a representation of the God's phallus. When used ceremonially, it pairs with the chalice to reenact the moment of creation, when the masculine and feminine aspects of universal source energy combine. The athame is also used to perform a number of tasks in each ritual. Some traditions hold that two athames of specific make are required in ceremony; a black-handled one that only cuts a handfasting cake and never draws blood (this one is also called a bolline), and a white-handled dagger that is used for all other ceremonial uses. However, most other traditions allow you to use whatever dagger calls to you, especially if it is tied to your path's cultural influence. The fine point of athames makes them ideal for directing energy, so in addition to cutting they are often used to open and close circles, to focus and guide energy, and to symbolize intention.

Wand

Wands are long rods of wood that are used to focus and direct energy in ritual. The wood used to make a wand is chosen specifically for its magickal properties, and many are adorned with metal, crystals, and symbols to further hone the magick inherent in the wand.

Incense

Incense is a grand representation of air that is usually carried around the circle when invoking the east and the element of air in circle-casting. It's also used for consecration, purifying items, and in spellwork. This item is placed near one of the illuminator candles, off to one side of the altar. There are several different types of incense. Incense sticks are the most commonly available on the market. They can be bought nearly everywhere, but you will want to make sure that they contain all-natural ingredients as opposed to synthetic fragrances.

Never buy blends that contain only fragrance oils. Your incense should have a comprehensive ingredient list that contains items like essential oils, ground herbs, and resin. You will also need an incense holder that you can easily stand your stick in. Look for one that catches ash for less mess, and less risk of burning holes in your altar cloth.

Incense cones are much like incense sticks. They're made of the same combustible material and burn slowly over a period of time. You will need a heat-proof dish that can catch ash for these as well, but they last a long time. The same rules apply with cone incense when shopping around: all-natural ingredients are the only way to go. Loose incense is generally the preferred type among Wiccans. These blends of dried and crumpled herbs and wood shavings are mixed with oils or small granules of resin. They are quite fun to use, and very easy to make. The only potential drawback is that you will need charcoal tablets to burn them on, as well as a very sturdy heat-proof dish or censer to place the charcoal in. Loose incense doesn't tend to burn for as long as other types, but it's got a very back-to-basics aesthetic since you can see literally every ingredient in the blend.

It's very important that loose, burning incense is not disturbed, since the smoldering bits of herbal oils and grounds can fairly easily ignite or burn holes in fabric and other surfaces. Loose incense also comes in powdered form, which is less unpredictable when burning, but tends to burn even faster than the traditional loose variety. Resins are another form of incense, which are not often found in shops that sell more conventional incense, but which have been used by Native Americans in their ceremonies for hundreds of years. These sticky bricks are made with sap, dried herbs, woods, and oils and have very strong and clean fragrances. They also require charcoal and other accessories, described in the following section.

Finally, smudge sticks, while not technically considered incense, can be used for the same purpose. They're made up of bundles of partially dried herbs that smolder well. The most common smudge sticks are made using sage, which is used in house cleansing and purification rites. When casting a circle, it's best to leave the stick smoldering in a heatproof dish and use a feather to fan the smoke around. This will prevent embers from randomly dropping to the floor and burning things. You can make your own smudge sticks too, using herbs that you think are most appropriate for your intended purpose for casting a circle or in devotion to a specific Sabbat. You will need to make sure that they do not contain any noxious chemicals that would be harmful to inhale, so do your research before experimenting with smudge sticks.

Note: some people prefer not to use incense due to allergies and asthma that can flare up due to certain mixtures of oils and herbs, or even just the smoke in general. If this is the case, you can light a candle anointed with oil that represents air, and this will at least help to signify air in some manner without irritating your lungs.

Book of Shadow

A book of shadows is a book or journal that records the wisdom and spells necessary to a witch's practice. A book of shadows can contain information on the magickal properties of herbs, trees, and crystals, it can record a witch's different experiences as he or she grows in the craft, and it can contain the recipes necessary for completing certain spells. Solitary practitioners will create their own book of shadows, while covens might compile their collective knowledge into a group book.

Chalice

A chalice is a ceremonial cup or goblet that represents the vulva and womb of the Goddess. Chalices can be made of stone or metal, usually silver. Chalices are usually used to hold the wine or ale in the ceremonial cakes and ale that close each ritual, though they may serve different uses depending on the spell. When paired with the athame, the chalice represents the feminine half of the act of creation.

Cakes and Plate

A cake plate can be any ordinary plate, or something special, like a piece of china. It should always be kept separate from any other dishes, bowls, and tools that touch anything inedible—like poisonous herbs, oils, incense, or other ingredients for spellwork. If you are on your own, you can use a small dish, but covens should get a large enough dish to hold an entire group's worth of cakes or other bite-size offerings. As for the "cakes" themselves, they don't really have to be cakes. Traditionally, witches would make oatcakes for this purpose, but you can make any sort of cookie or biscuit, or use fruit instead, or even chop up some veggies if that's more your style.

Covens may have their own preferences according their traditions (and any allergies), but solitary practitioners can go for whatever they feel comfortable with offering up. The cakes sit on the same side of the altar as the chalice, ready for when the ritual is nearing its end. It's often nice to simply enjoy your Cakes and Ale in quiet introspection. It can also be fun to sit and enjoy music and trance during the moments of thanks.

Dush of Water

Water is always kept on hand in a ritual to represent the water element. Witches always advocate for the use of natural spring water in ceremony, either from a nearby river or stream, from the ocean, or from a bottled source. Many spells also call for the use of water charged with the energy of the full moon, the new moon, or the sun.

Dish of Sea

Another small dish on the surface of your altar will contain your earth representation. This can be soil, sea salt, or even small pebbles, which is a really nice touch for outdoor rituals. You can sprinkle the sea salt or soil as you walk around the circle and invoke the earth element and the northern Watchtower. (Note: Whichever you use, you may want to sweep or vacuum it up once you've closed your circle, especially if you have pets.) Like the water dish, this vessel should be kept for the one purpose only.

Salt

Salt is used to represent the earth element in ritual. Blessed salt that is mixed with scented oils is often used to create a boundary in sacred space, or it can be used to cleanse an area or an item. Salt is often mixed with water in ceremony to represent the two feminine elements together.

Pentacle

There are so many options for wearing the pentacle that it is not funny. You can even have it printed on shoes. If you have the pentacle printed on your shoes and sewn into your robe, you do not need jewelry covered in pentacles. You can save the jewelry for gemstones that will help the ritual spell of the night you are celebrating.

Chapter 4: Wicca Moon Magic

The Triple Goddess

The goddess herself is thought to be comprised of three main aspects, the maiden, mother, and crone. This is syncretized with the fact that the divine feminine mirrors humanity's ability to create life, and as such, life is often marked by certain milestones: childhood, coming-of-age, motherhood, reaching maturity, and the wisdom of age.

Regardless of the aspects of fertility, childbirth, and procreation, the triple goddess and her three forms have meaning and messages for everyone, young or old, regardless of gender.

A popular symbol for Wiccans and often used in jewelry is the symbol for the triple goddess: a full moon bracketed by a waning and waxing crescent.

The Mother

The Mother is the second form of the Goddess. When the Moon becomes full, The Mother symbol takes over, depicting the abundance that is present on the Earth. She is also associated with the season of Summer, when the animals and plants are filled with life and there is a sense of "lushness" in the air. Many Wiccans and Witches believe that The Mother form is the most powerful aspect of the Goddess.

The Mother aspect of the goddess is the most commonly-worshipped aspect. Here we see the goddess as giver and sustainer of life, providing us with abundance, nourishment, motherly healing, and empathy, as well as stern guidance when we need it. Some mother goddesses are sweet, patient and kind, others are also loving but firmer, directing us to the proper path to ensure our utmost happiness.

In this aspect, the goddess becomes the well-spring of life and the provider. She is at her highest physical power, represented by the height of summer and the laden fruit trees, and tall, waving crops of grains. The Mother brings balance and a sense of satisfaction to us—life is abundant, we are worthy of happiness, and all is well.

The color red is associated with the Mother goddess as it obviously conveys the blood of the menstrual cycle and of the womb. She gives us her lifeblood that we may carry on our own bloodlines. Blue is another color associated with the Mother goddess, as with Yemaya, a beloved goddess of the ocean worshipped in Nigeria, the Americas, and the Caribbean. Animals beloved to the Mother are pregnant animals, the dove, and deer.

While the Maiden is more of an inspirer, cohort, and adventure companion, the Mother goddess is here to guide us in life and often help us make difficult decisions. Just like a mother, she wants what is best for us, and seeks to show us the way in moments of miraculous, loving kindness. When we feel like we can't go any further, the Mother goddess will draw near, allows us to cry against her mantle of stars, and soothe our pains and hurts while inspiring us to draw more strength and soldier on.

She will work with you to avoid the pitfalls of addiction and excess. You will see clearly within her light what changes you need to make in your life to bring happiness, harmony, and peace to your days, as well as your nights.

The Mother goddess is most powerful during the full moon. Perform magic for abundance, self-love, healing, and personal strength when calling to the Mother goddess. Ask for her help with marriage, childbirth and fertility, life partners, caring for your animals and garden, making important life decisions, and help with awakening your natural spirituality.

The sabbaths of Beltane, Litha, and Lammas are sacred to the goddess in her Mother aspect.

Some Mother goddesses are: Bast, Ceres, Corn Mother, Frigg, Hathor, Isis, Macha, and Venus.

Esbats

In addition to the eight sabbaths of Yule, Imbolc, Ostara, Beltane, Litha, Lammas, Mabon, and Samhain, there are what Wiccans call esbats or the lunar celebrations that follow the ever-changing phases of the moon. The esbats can be considered a second Wheel of the Year and while not every pagan follows them, they present many opportunities for ritual and magic outside of the major sabbaths.

During an esbat, the focus is, of course, the moon, and the goddess—particularly the aspect of the Triple Goddess. Communities and covens will often focus on one of the three aspects of the triple goddess for a lunar ceremony depending on the time of the year, such as the Crone aspect of the goddess in Autumn and Winter, the maiden aspect in Spring, and the Mother in late Spring and Summer.

Do not feel that you need to bring a specific deity into your sacred space if you are a solitary practitioner and wish to do magical work during an esbat. You may simply honor the goddess in general, and that is completely acceptable.

Most covens and communities celebrate one monthly esbat during that month's full moon, but an esbat can be observed at any time.

The Crone

Finally, we have the Crone, which is represented by the waning of the moon and indicates death. Most people think of this symbol as a reference to the end. However, what The Crone is showing is the wisdom that is gained by living a life fully. When it comes to the seasons, she is represented by Autumn and Winter, showing the end of the growing season and the prelude to a new season. This cycle begins again with the appearance of The Maiden and the Spring season.

Power of the Moon

It gives me great pleasure to present these 'instructions' and ask that you use them to bring about whatever it is you want from your life. Before I do so can I offer the following information for your consideration.

To give a brief explanation: the Moon points to a basic emotional need. Remember this, for it will help you understand your needs rather than your wants. For example: Moon in Cancer gives the emotional need for home and family, in Taurus for roots and stability.

These are needs and when understood can help cope with those moments of depression (which the Moon also rules) when your needs are not being met. Have you ever wanted something and couldn't afford it yet bought it anyway? This is your Sun sign talking to you (the Sun rules the ego).

Have you ever felt absolutely happy with your lot in life? This is the Moon talking to you for she is supplying your needs. Sure, they'll always be fluctuations (we all know about the phases of the Moon) but once you understand your needs versus your wants they will always be met.

In understanding this know in your heart that the Moon will always supply whatever it is you need.

On or near the New Moon you need to do some 'imagining.' First of all consider the following: Are we the master's of our own fate or, mere actor's playing to a script written long before we were born? Remember: A person's inner development and growth is subject to his or her own free will and your attitude to things 'inner' is the first step in mastering outside events for it's not what happens to you it's how you react to them.

Know it or not we're all born to a certain predestined set of outside circumstances (a jockey for example would not make a good basketball player and vice versa) that we can master by our inner attitude. This can and does bring positive or negative reactions.

By changing our inner attitude we can bring about changes in our outer conditions. This is a fact of life we must never, never forget. Your state of being attracts into your life whatever you dwell upon. If you think negative you will attract negative. If you think positive you will attract positive, there is no other way.

Another example: a stove is built for cooking, but what gets cooked is a matter of choice. Look at your Sun Sign for if you are a Pisces there's no point in trying to be a Sagittarian for the structure is different. Sure, you can incorporate certain Sagittarian traits but you are still a Pisces (or whatever sign you are). "You are who you are."

The New Moon is all about 'emergence' and soon you will surface from the dark into the light with no idea as to what is in store for you yet, possessing an inner confidence of knowing that whatever lies ahead is meant for you. Do not attempt to make things happen nor judge what is happening to you. Accept the experience of your 'birth.'

The following should be your one thought for the day: I am what I am and what is meant for me will not go past me. I accept all that is given to me no matter what it may be for the universe gives not one 'gram' more of what I am capable of carrying. Consider the word emergency and where it came from for the New Moon is all about urgency, a quickening and a new beginning. This is the 1st step on your journey towards life and living.

As you move through the days until the 1st quarter passing through the crescent phase to the 1st quarter you'll be laying the GROUNDWORK and putting into action whatever you come to realize needs to be done. In laying the groundwork take a few moments to briefly review the past. Don't dwell upon the past but realize it brought you to where you are now.

It's time to recognize this link and to assert your individuality. Learn from the past and from what you have learnt apply this wisdom to the future, for these days are 'future-oriented' yet you must still retain a consideration of the past. In living these few days, in accepting whatever they bring you, in acknowledging all that is happening to you is meant for you, an 'emergence' an idea or, a pathway to the future will reveal itself.

At the first quarter ACTION is the keyword. Whatever you've come to realize over the past few days you must put into action. This is a crisis or quickening phase and there'll be some pain experienced if you've not laid the groundwork or, a goal ahead to be reached if you have.

Working with the Lunar Cycle

A person's horoscope is heavily influenced by the Moon. The location of the beautiful Moon and that link that lays between the Moon and the Sun is definatenaly one of the main influences. It explains a person's feelings (emotional).

When you look at the Moon to determine the mood of a person you have to look for the cycle the Moon were in at the time of birth of the person.

Was the Moon, New, Crescent, First Quarter, Gibbous, Full, Disseminating, Last Quarter, or Balsamic Moon. These are called "the Lunar Cycle" and they can help you understand the moods of a person.

By finding the placement of the Moon in your chart you will be able to clarify why a person may have certain moods and often get into similar situations without realizing why.

For instance if your Moon were in the New Moon phase which last about three and a half days then your mood would generally be one of emergency.

The New Moon is for planting and creating. So the kind of mood for this person would be one of hopefulness for the future and generally perceive the world as a place of possibilities and a life of joy.

The next lunar cycle is The Crescent Moon and the person with the Moon in this position has a strong urge to overcome pressure and inertia of the karmic past and by working through these issues they often discover personal limits and their special purpose. This position is from three and a half to seven days after New Moon.

The Gibbous Moon phase is ten and a half to fourteen days after New Moon and with this position you have an intense energy of overcoming past and present issues. You believe that whatever decisions have been made must now be lived with. This is a time of testing and adjustment, flexibility and perseverance are qualities that need to be nurtured.

Third Quarter or Full Moon is when it is opposite the Sun. This position has to do with your relationships of the heart, marriage and is a constant feeling of insecurity in which you may wonder if your partner is really happy with you. Learn to be happy within yourself and do not let your partner control your moods.

Next is the Disseminating phase which is three and a half to seven days after the Full Moon. This is a time where you begin to understand your inner struggle and are able to let go of them because you now understand what is underneath them.

The Last Quarter is seven to ten and a half days after full Moon. This position represents the harvest and meaning of understanding and whatever does not harmonize with the growing consciousness and understanding cannot be accepted.

The last phase is the Balsamic which occurs during the final eight of the entire cycle ten and a half to fourteen days after the Full Moon. The general mood of this cycle is release and a period when emptying is necessary before a new cycle can begin.

The Balsamic Moon people are old souls who have lived before and are here to complete and put into use those gifts they have already attained hence fulfilling a past vision.

New Moon

When the New Moon reveals itself in the sky, it means that the Mother Goddess is present during the infant stage in her life. This is symbolic for the fact that it represents new beginnings, hope, growth, introductions, faith, sowing seeds, and optimism. This is why magick that leads you towards the introduction of something is best performed during this moon phase. Ideally, you should be making a spell within the first three days since the presence of the new moon.

Waxing Moon

The new moon has a unique energy that is often felt by those who are sensitive to changes in the air. It is a time for beginnings, for embarking on new voyages, actual or symbolic. It pushes the individual forward whether they are willing or not. A new moon might cause sleeplessness or emotional reactions. It is letting us know that the full moon is on its way, and with that, shifting tides within our hearts and within our spirits.

The new moon is representative of the Maiden aspect of the goddess. This aspect reflects apprenticeship, students, learning and studies as well as the hunter aspect of the goddess-like we see in Artemis. The Maiden is not always aromantic, however, and the new moon can also signal new love and the first signs of romance. The new moon is not only for beginnings, but second attempts, ascending to the next level of something, and breakthrough achievements.

Magic suitable for the new moon includes commitments to new starts, blessings for a new job, home, course of study, or relationship. Money magic started on the new moon and culminating on the full moon is especially potent. A simple candle spell: anoint a green candle with money drawing oil, and light it each night at 7PM, 8PM, or 9PM. Spend seven minutes meditating and imagining money coming to you happily, joyfully—do not wonder how or why. On the full moon, allow the candle to burn completely and tell the universe you are ready to receive abundance.

Full Moon

The full moon is the most potent time to perform magic. Its power naturally increases any witchcraft that is performed. In addition, this is the time most covens and communities choose to celebrate their monthly esbat, honoring the goddess in whichever aspect is best mirrored by the season. Sometimes, naming ceremonies, also called wiccanings, and hand-fastings, Wiccan versions of marriage ceremonies, are performed during a full moon esbat. This way, their special day is performed on an auspicious day but will not conflict with community ceremonies or worship during more important sabbaths.

The full moon becomes a powerful light that shines upon us, which is bringing many things into focus and up to the surface. It is a powerful time for self-reflection and revelation. The full moon asks of us to be honest with ourselves, but also to be gentle and empathetic. The moon is the goddess incarnate, loving and nurturing, ancient and wise. The goddess wants us to be happy and fulfilled. Turning to her in times of questioning can reveal possibilities you didn't know existed.

Any magic and spell is suitable for the full moon, naturally increased in efficacy and strength. Because of the full moon's ability to reveal truths to ourselves, however, any magic that adversely affects another person should be avoided, because the Rules of Three and Return will be increased, too. A Wiccan chooses to create greater peace and harmony in the world and doesn't actively choose to add to the world's strife or pain. Attend to your magic during the full moon with a loving, humble heart and you will receive great returns.

Half Moon

Sometimes, the act of letting go means accepting the fact that we have a few traits within us that we are not particularly proud of and are hesitant to accept. This spell will help you come to terms with these traits and allow you to see yourself in a different light.

Waning Moon

When the moon enters its waning stages, then the Mother Goddess is said to be entering the crone stage of her life. Most people associate old age with negative aspects such as weakness, death, sickness, and loneliness. But in the case of the Goddess, it reflects a life well spent, wisdom accumulated over the years, a period of cleansing, and a chance to be reborn.

Dark Moon

The dark moon's energy can be unsettling for some. Like the full moon, the dark moon is a mirror of the self, though it shows us our shadow side rather than the side the world sees day to day. A concept of a shadow self in Wiccan and other pagan faiths is that we all have darker leanings, habits, responses, or traits that we may not be proud of, or even ashamed of. However, the god and goddess support us as being our authentic selves as humans. They teach us that being human is nothing to be ashamed of.

Sometimes our shadows, when properly understood, accepted, and controlled, can be some of our strongest features. Doing shadow work under a dark moon is a way to courageously explore one's self, and come to terms with it, thus emerging stronger, happier, and more complete.

Magic to be performed on a dark moon may involve protection, invisibility, drawing the truth out from obscurity, raising self-confidence, accepting one's shadow traits, forgiveness of one's self or of another, making a pact to strive for something, and banishing negative energy from one's person, life, or home.

Blue Moon

A blue moon is a second full moon in a month and presents a wonderful opportunity to perform magic that focuses on good fortune and luck. The blue moon increases the full moon's potency even more so nearly any magic focusing on positivity and gain should be performed at this time.

Lunar eclipses

This is as a result of something called a syzygy where the Earth, Sun, and Moon are almost exactly in line with each other. As the Earth moves between the other two heavenly bodies, its shadow appears on the Moon. This shadow is called an umbra.

Lunar eclipse is when a level 5 red eclipse occurs. The illusion of the red color is caused by the Earth's shadow and presents an interesting time to perform magical spells. As the blood moon is the result of the Sun, Moon, and Earth joining forces, so to speak, so we can focus on spells that address our outer selves, inner knowledge and intuition, and how we are grounded in knowledge and experience. Breakthrough spells for career, a new book deal, meeting the lover of your dreams, overcoming a physical impairment, or any epiphany regarding self-awareness can be cast during a blood moon. Who knows—you might just win the lottery! Just give it a try.

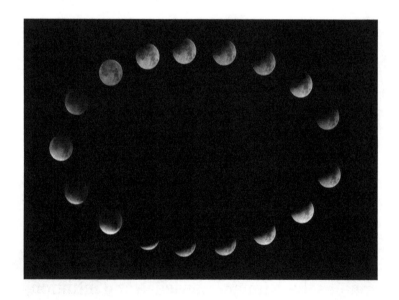

Part 2: Chapter 5: Crystals and Other Mineral Stones

Crystals and stones are powerful items for magic for those who resonate with these Earth energies. They all have different correspondences to planets, elements, and herbs. Each stone also has specific purposes that it helps with, so before you purchase stones, it can be useful to do some research—there are many books and online resources like the this book that you are reading now, detailing crystals and their magical properties. The magical power of stone has been recognized by people all over the world from as far back as 11,000 years ago, when the oldest known stone temple was built at Göbekli Tepe in Turkey.

The famous sites of Stonehenge, Newgrange, and other monuments in Europe and beyond are further testaments to our long history of relationship with this most fundamental building block provided by the Earth. Stone's ability to shelter our early ancestors surely had something to do with the importance it held in the spiritual lives of the communities who built these mysterious structures. To this day, cairns— or piles of stones—are still used as landmarks on trails and coastlines, as well as memorials to the deceased and tributes to the unseen spirits of the natural world. Then there is the widespread tradition of making, carrying, and/or giving away "wishing stones," which are small enough to be carried in pockets and often have words like "love," "peace," and "luck" carved into them.

But there are certain treasures sourced from the Earth that hold particular power for contemporary spiritual seekers, including Wiccans and other Pagans. Because healing physical, emotional, and spiritual is often a goal of magic, there is quite a bit of overlap between what alternative healers know about crystals and stones, and what Witches know. Furthermore, it might be argued that crystals and stones are more suited for healing magic than non-natural objects, such as candles (though magic for healing can certainly involve candles or any other object).

Because of this overlap, the word "healing" will show up often in this guide, and much of the information about the magical uses of specific crystals will include their use in healing. However, this information is in no way intended to replace that which a trained practitioner in the alternative healing modalities would provide, and should not be used in place of needed medical treatment of any kind.

The focus of this guide is on the use of crystals and mineral stones in magic, and will therefore pay more attention to the emotional and spiritual elements of their unique and special powers. Of course, in Wiccan tradition, the use of crystals goes well beyond healing. Indeed, they are often involved in many facets of spiritual and magical practice. Crystals and stones are commonly used for making the circle the ritual is being performed in sacred regardless it's being used by a coven or a witch. Gods and goddess are honored by use of crystal and stones to particular deities.

Keeping touch with the changing tradition, they are also used in talismans, amulets and for protection.

Some magical tools, such as wands and pentacles, are decorated with crystals, and they can also be used to improve the energy of any indoor or outdoor space. Finally, crystals and stones can be and are powerful components when we talk of spellwork, which is the focus of this guide. Before getting into any further detail, however, it's helpful to take a brief look at the terminology associated with crystals and other stones in order to get a better understanding of the physical makeup of these mysterious gifts from the Earth.

Chapter 6: Introduction to Mineral Stones and Crystals

From the deep waters of documented history, people are charmed in the exquisite beauty of naturally befalling crystals originating deep down below the Earth. People from the ancient days in countries such as Egypt, Rome, Greece, China, India, Japan, Central and South America crystals to them were used not just in jewelry and amulets, but also in the religious art, healing and weaponry. Over the past Number of decades, popularity of the energy and ability of crystals in the art of healing and also the magical arts has observed renaissance.

This guide explores the use of crystals from the standpoint of Witches and Wiccans, fair enough you do not need to see yourself as a witch or even a Wiccan to profit from the energy of stone and crystals. This guide provides an overview of the many uses of crystals in healing and magic and the underlying principles of the Universal forces that make it all work. You'll learn about the physical makeup of these amazing pieces of the Earth, and also learn about energetic and unique vibrations that may hey you as a Wiccan to consciously bring out the reality perspective of your day today life on the emotional, spiritual and physical planes.

You'll be introduced to thirteen (13) of the utmost popular and accessible crystals and mineral stones and their primary uses, as well as instructions on how to care for and charge them. Finally, you'll find a number of spells and the magical workings centered around crystals, providing a variety of magical solutions to everyday issues. Remember that with any kind of magic, repeated practice is what leads to success. So be persistent as you work to incorporate your new knowledge, and be certain to allow the crystals and stones guide you in your process, as they make wonderful guides on the spiritual path.

In many "new age" and Wiccan circles, the word "crystal" talks about a large variety of minerals and many of them aren't even true crystals. All of them fall under the crystal umbrella.

A simple definition of a mineral is "any inorganic substance that gets formed in the

Earth's underground geological processes naturally." Each mineral will have its own energy signature and chemical composition.

Most minerals are made of molecules that fit together in repeating patterns, that gives them their geometric forms that we think of when we hear "crystal." When crystals form, it is called crystallization. Crystals form when liquids cool and begin to harden. Specific molecules in this liquid will band together while they try to stabilize themselves. This happens in a repeating and uniform pattern that creates the crystal. Crystals can be formed from magma, or liquid rock, when it cools off. If it cools very slowly, crystals form. Very valuable crystals like emeralds, rubies, and diamonds will form like this.

The most common crystal is the clear quartz. This is what a true crystal ball will be made of. Amethyst and rose quartz follow the clear quartz as the most abundant. Bloodstone, jade, and lapis lazuli are popular stones that are used in magic. These crystals are actually combinations of minerals and aren't considered to be true crystals. Some crystals like jet and amber are actually organic substances that have been fossilized. In order to keep things simple, many people will work with these gifts will use the words "stones" and "crystals" interchangeably.

The Faces and Shapes of Crystals

Crystals are easily recognized by their shape. They consist of sharp angles and flat faces. These shapes aren't necessary for crystals, but the shape is usually there and easy to see.

Crystals that have well-formed flat faces are called euhedral crystals. Crystals that are anhedral don't because the crystal will be just one grain in a polycrystalline solid.

The facets of the euhedral crystal are stacked in a certain pattern relative to the crystal's atomic arrangement. This happens because some surfaces are more stable than the others. As the crystal gets larger, now atoms will attach themselves to the rougher parts of the surface but won't to the flat surfaces. This causes the flat surfaces to grow smoother and larger, until the entire surface of the crystal consists of these surfaces.

The most common and oldest technique in crystallography measures the three-dimensional orientation of the crystal faces and uses them to infer the crystal's symmetry.

The habit of a crystal is its external shape. This gets determined by the structure of the crystal, the bonding, and chemistry of the crystal, and the conditions present when the crystal was formed.

Crystals Properties

Crystals will have flat surfaces that are called facets. They can form many shapes like squares, rectangles, and triangles. These shapes are results of the kind of atoms and molecules that are in the crystal. Large and small crystals that are created from the same molecules will have similar shapes.

There are seven basic shapes of crystals that are called lattices. These are monoclinic, tetragonal, hexagonal, orthorhombic, triclinic, trigonal, and cubic.

Choosing and preparing your crystals

Most people familiar with crystal magick will tell you that you do not choose the crystal – the crystal chooses you. As with all magick, let your intuition be your guide. Begin with whatever colors or types of crystal you feel most drawn to. When shopping for crystals, try to handle them if possible. Pick them up and hold them to get a feel for it. Pay attention to the types of sensations, thoughts, or feelings it evokes.

You may receive positive thoughts or feelings, or you could get a warm tingly sensation in your hand when holding a particular crystal. These are all good signs that the crystal is a good fit for you.

Once you get your crystals, it is important to cleanse them. Crystals absorb and hold onto energies they come into contact with, which can clog up the crystals' natural energies and keep them from working at their full potential. It is very important that you cleanse any crystals you will work with. This should be done upon first obtaining them, and periodically throughout the year, particularly after you use them in a spell or for chakra or healing work. Cleansing is quite simple to do and there are a variety of ways to do this, based upon the type of crystals you have and your own personal preferences.

Cleansing

Water Bath – A water bath is one of the more common methods for cleansing crystals, however please keep in mind that many crystals can break down or be damaged by prolonged exposure to water. If you choose to use this method, it should only be done with nonporous and nonmetallic crystals, such as Quartz, Agate, or Aventurine.

To cleanse your crystals this way, fill a glass bowl with enough water to cover your crystals. Some people advise adding in sea salt to the water, but please be aware that salt water is even more corrosive than plain water and can potentially damage your crystals or change their appearance.

Place your crystals into the water and let them soak for thirty minutes to an hour. When they are finished, pour the water out. If it is plain water, you can poor it into the earth outside. If it is salt water, I recommend pouring it down the sink to avoid damaging plant life with the salt.

➤ Please be aware that water can dissolve certain crystals, breaking them down or eating away at the surface. Water and salt water can both change the color and appearance of your crystals. Some crystals can even release toxins when wet. ALWAYS USE CAUTION WHEN USING CRYSTALS NEAR OR IN WATER.

Personally, I do not like cleansing my crystals in water (and especially salt water) for this reason. I prefer to use a combination of smudging and visualization, which I detail below.

Visualization – This is a simple method that requires nothing but your crystal and a quiet place to focus. Simply hold your crystal between your hands and visualize a white light forming. Feel this pure white energy warm the crystal and cleanse it of any negative or unwanted energy. Keep up the visualization for as long as it takes for you to feel that the crystal is purified.

Smudging – This is also a very popular method for cleansing anything from crystals, to magickal tools, to a room or your entire house. Simply light some incense and pass the crystals through the smoke to cleanse them. It doesn't take long, a few passes through the smoke should be enough. Visualize the smoke cleansing and purifying the crystals while you smudge them.

*Sage and Sandalwood are both popular choices for purification, but others will work just as well – check the reference guide at the end of this book for a list of other purification herbs.

Moonlight – This method is best done on a full moon, but that isn't strictly necessary. You do, however, want to make sure that the moon is full enough to put out a decent amount of light. The closer to the full moon you are, the stronger the cleansing energy. To cleanse your crystals using this method, simply leave them out overnight on a window ledge or somewhere that the moonlight can reach them. The energy of the moon will gently cleanse your crystals of any unwanted energies. Make sure to move your crystals the next morning, however, as prolonged exposure to sunlight can fade or alter some crystals.

Amethyst Cluster or Amethyst Geode – This is similar to the moonlight method, however with this you will use the energy of an Amethyst cluster or a geode to gently cleanse your crystals. As Amethyst has the natural ability to absorb negative energy and release positive energy, placing your crystals inside an Amethyst geode or on top of an Amethyst cluster will purify your crystals of undesirable energies. I recommend leaving your crystals on the

Amethyst for about 24 hours to make sure it is fully cleansed.

Chapter 7: Incorporating Crystals Into Your Life

Even though they are classified as inorganic, crystals are understood by most healers and Witches to be living because they give healing energy to plants, animals, and people. Specific crystals like tourmaline and quartz exhibit a power that scientists call "the piezoelectric effect." When pressure is applied to these stones, like being tapped with a hammer or squeezing them, they will give off an electric charge. Crystals like quartz exhibit a pyroelectricity. This means they release an electric charge when they get exposed to a temperature change.

Crystals are made up of minerals that are in a structured, geometric pattern. They have been classified according to their internal structures. It is their geometrical structure that gives them the healing and magical properties.

The crystal's power comes from its internal geometry. To be able to completely understand this, you have to understand sacred geometry. This is a philosophical and mathematical field the looks at the proportions and geometrical shapes within the Universe. These can be found anywhere in the world. It can be found in man-made buildings and nature. According to this, every geometric shape will vibrate with its own frequency and this gives them their specific energetic properties. The symbols vary and are numerous: the Pentacle, the Triskele, the Flower of Life, and the Fibonacci spiral just to name a few.

Because gemstones are arranged naturally in a geometric pattern, sacred geometry will also apply to them. This theory is the core of crystal magic. This is why we build grids using geometric shapes.

Know that you know about sacred geometry, it will help you understand how and why crystals work. Every crystal will vibrate at a frequency that is unique to their internal structure. These vibrations will affect the crystal's energy in ways that science can't explain. Because we are energy, we can be affected by crystals. Because crystals vibrated at high frequencies, they naturally store information. This is why quartz and selenite are used in electronic devices. With intentions, we can program and charge crystals so that they can help us manifest our goals. They are batteries that help power our intentions. This makes them perfect for use in magic.

There are actually only a few crystals that are popular enough to be used in magic and healing that has shown these effects during scientific studies. Normal science hasn't discovered what alternative healing practitioners have always known and that is each crystal gives off its own energy that will interact with the energy and everything that is around it.

Witches along with Wiccans know that a stone or crystals' power is the same power that is in natural phenomena like a flowing river or the wind. Everything whether invisible or visible is nothing but energy. All of that energy is connected. Because intention or thought is also energy, this too can be harnessed and sent into the Universe through the crystals that we work with. By doing this, the stones and crystals become energy conduits. They can bring healing to us or send positive energy into the spiritual realm to manifest change in the lives of others as well as ourselves.

Chapter 8: How Does Crystal Magic Work?

Crystal magic, like any other form of magic, is essentially the art of directing a specific intention into the Universe at the spiritual level in order to effect change on the material plane. While crystal spellwork may make use of other tools, such as candles, herbs, charms, chants, etc., the main "ingredient" of this kind of magic will be one or more crystals or other mineral stones. Crystals are a unique magical tool in that they occur in nature and they are not made by human hands like candles, cauldrons, athames and wands.

They can be polished and carved into beautiful shapes, but are just as effective when left "raw" in their original state. Even scientists speak of the process of crystal formation as "growing," since crystals start out small and then increase in size as new atoms are added to their structures under the Earth's surface. The shape, size, and color of a given crystal's formation will depend on the temperature, location, and presence of other minerals, as part of an ancient and ongoing dynamic process of creation. If you have come into contact with a crystal touched and probably held it in your hand and turned it a number of angles, you have certainly felt those breathtaking mysterious feel of wonder they evoke. You can feel the tendency of them speaking in silence of the creative, infinite and the living power possessed by the earth.

Wiccans and some of the Witches have the belief that the power or force of crystals and mineral stones is also paramount the same as power inherent in some other natural phenomena, for instance as a flowing river or even the wind. I this case all matter, visible and the invisible, is energy, and all this energy/force is interconnected.

This core concept is found in both metaphysics and quantum physics, and while the exact ways in which energy communicates and ultimately transforms reality remain a mystery, we can use the power of our intentions in conjunction with the power of crystals to harness this interconnectedness of the Universe, both on the material and the spiritual plane.

Some healers who use crystals theorize that the stones' healing abilities stem from their piezoelectric and pyroelectric qualities, but in reality just a small number of crystals are most often used in magic and healing are known to exhibit these effects. Nonetheless, every crystal gives very its own and unique subtle energy which then go on to interact with other the energy fields around its environs. Therefore, every crystal responds to the energy flowing through the human body, and when used appropriately helps to balance that flow and restore it to optimal conditions for good health.

Another way to view this concept of energy is through the Hermetic principle of the Law of Vibration, which states that all matter is in constant motion, even though most of it appears to be perfectly still. At the subatomic level, everything is moving and therefore interacting with everything else. The rate, or frequency, at which any particular piece of matter is vibrating will determine how we perceive it with our senses, just like how its energy interacts with ours.

Each crystal vibrates at its own precise frequency, which is determined by its physical makeup, and will affect other matter, such as the human body, in a particular way through these vibrations. The frequency of a particular crystal will also resonate with the frequencies of a particular condition or situation in life that we wish to change or manifest. For example, rose quartz resonates with the frequencies of friendship and love, and is therefore used in spellwork for these aims.

Colors are also the vibrations of the light, and coexist well with different perspectives of our being that is love, money matters and health as per their specific energetic vibrations. Color of a stone will therefore often have a correspondence with particular magical aims. Rose quartz which bare color pink with presence of harmonizing energetic loving vibration. The color and the physical makeup of this kind of quartz combine to construct a powerful energy for bringing love your life. Similarly, green is the color that has got vibrational resonance in abundance. Therefore, some stones which are green, such as bloodstone, are to be a little bit more specific they are best for spellwork for matters to do with prosperity.

However, traditional color associations such as those used in candle magic are not always a key factor in crystal-centered magic. For example, citrine and pyrite, both primarily yellow in color, are highly associated with prosperity and wealth. Finally, one more way to view the basic makeup of all matter in the Universe is as information, or consciousness. The Hermetic principle of the Law of Mentalism states that at the basic level, everything is mental, that all of creation stems from the Universal mind. Since thought is energy, the power of thought can shape our reality. It has been established that positive thoughts raise the frequency of one's energetic vibration, while negative thoughts lower it.

We can harness this power of thought and use it to send our intentions out straight into the universe via the force or energy field (of the crystals and stones chosen to function with. Crystals and stones are conduits of energy in this form. Both of them can bring about healing energy, and at the same time send the positive energy towards the spiritual realm and result to manifest and real dynamic changes in life. Understanding what crystals are and why they make such great magical tools is the first step toward learning how to use them to manifest positive change in your life.

If you're reading this guide, you may already have one or more crystals in your possession, or you may just be simply feeling drawn to learn more about them. In order to work crystal magic, you'll need at least one, though a good handful of a few different types is ideal. In the next section, you'll find tips on choosing and caring for your crystals, as well as exercises and ideas for building a relationship with them for effective use in magic. We'll also take a closer look at 13 common crystals and mineral stones and their magical uses. If you're undecided as to what kind of crystal to begin with, this information can help you narrow down your choices.

Chapter 9: Projective Stones

Projective energies are and can be compared to the yang energy or power of the system of the Chinese. These are powerful (masculine) energies, that are often characterized as feeling or being strong, physical, bright, active, hot and electric. Colors such as red, orange, yellow and gold, are affiliated with projective stones and tend to be resonate with sunlight. They often bring out a "charged or energized" feeling, which can probably range from subtle all the way to quite "buzzy," and that is depending on the kind of stone and also the level of receptivity of the individual holding it.

It's important to note also that projective stones are best suited stones for the magic involving protection from negative energy and also healing. Projective stones are associated or affiliated with the powerful Elements of Air and Fire, bringing the aspect of choices for working for courage, vitality, and intellectual power. They (Projective stones) influence the conscious mind, they are good to have in possession when you're feeling the need for strength, will power, determination, or self-confidence. We have some popular projective stones which include amber, carnelian, bloodstone, citrine, red jasper, garnet, tiger's eye and onyx.

Chapter 10: Receptive Stones

Receptive energies can sure be said to corresponsive with the yin energy known to be of Chinese system, and are put into context as powerful feminine energies, of which they might be experienced as inward, calm, spiritual, magnetic, cold and passive. The colors associated with receptive stones are attractive cool colors, for example green, purple, blue, grey and silver. (Pink stones, given that they are toward the start of color spectrum, they too are also receptive generally, as the pink color is more of calming than energizing in comparison orange or red.)

By having a receptive stone in possession of your hand is almost a guarantee that it will make you feel calmer, making you feel like the stone is absorbing that feel of anxiety from your body. Compared with projective stones, this kind of effect usually do vary from one stone to the other stone and an individual to an individual. The receptive stones are affiliated with the aspect of feminine Elements of the Water and Earth, They (receptive stones) are perfect for emotional, meditation and physical grounding, and also promoting the psychic abilities. They work out great on the human subconscious mind, they might be instrumental for spellwork for, compassion, love, spiritual development and peace. Some of the receptive stones do include malachite, jade moonstone, rose quartz, opal, and turquoise.

Chapter 11: Different Types of Crystals and Their Applications

The Earth has produced a truly stunning variety of crystals and other mineral stones, many, many of which are wonderful tools in healing and magic. Below is an introduction to 13 of the most popular and versatile stones used in various magical traditions around the world. Think of this group of stones as a sort of "Witch's starter kit" for crystal magic! Remember, there's no need to go out and buy one of each kind of stone all at once, but, if you find yourself overwhelmed by the choices when you do seek to acquire a stone or two, you can use this list to help make a decision. Here, you'll find information on each stone's appearance, key energetic properties, and common magical uses.

Quartz Crystal

The most abundant and arguably the most versatile crystal on the planet, quartz is the one most people associate with the word "crystal."

Crystal originated from the Quartz, crystal which comes from the Greek people "krystallos," which means "clear ice." Greeks used to believe that quartz crystal (clear) was ice that deities formed from celestial water could not. Clear quartz is a supreme aid in concentration, fostering intellectual clarity, new ideas, and strengthened focus. It increases awareness, helps with memory and filters out external distractions.

Interestingly, it is both helpful for sleep and for raising energy, as it has a somewhat hypnotic quality but also contains the full spectrum of light, which is seen when it's used as a prism.

Quartz is a great purifier, helping to eliminate negativity and restore positive energy in a person or in one's surroundings. It's useful in meditation and clearing out inner turmoil, replacing it with positive feelings and affirmations. It assists with perseverance and patience, bringing a sense of purpose and harmony to those who work with its energy. Clear quartz is a very versatile stone, easy to "program" (or charge) with magical intention for any positive purpose. It stores and concentrates the energy, retaining it for use in healing and magic at a later time. This crystal serves to amplify the power of your intentions, as well as the power of other stones used along with it in ritual. It is particularly well-suited for communication with spirit guides, building psychic ability, communication with animals and plants, and recalling past lives. Many people use quartz in workings connected to strengthening intuition and spiritual development. It also works well for attracting love and prosperity.

Wearing or carrying a clear quartz crystal helps keep personal energy strong and positive, and the mind and heart open to guidance from the higher realms. It dispels negative energy from others in your environment. Placing quartz in the bath is a good way to unwind and clear your mind when facing confusing events.

Key words: Clarity, Transformation, Manifestation

Zodiac Sign: Leo

Planet: Sun

Element: Fire

Rose Quartz

This crystal is pink in color it is believed to carry very soothing and gentle energy that gives a feeling of comfort to those wounded. The pink colored gemstone can and is believed to give treatment to those suffering emotionally and also serves as a natural remedy to heartsick. Giving an example, rose quartz serves the following.

Encourages self-love, Releases repressed hurts, Heals emotional body, Relieves loneliness, Eases heartache, offers inner peace, Promotes forgiveness. For acceptance and self-love, rose quartz gives you room and space to be and get in touch with in basic self. Basically it allows you to love your inner self and to appreciate the beauty that comes with it. It gives you the license to communicate with the inner spirits in you, regardless of your awareness about them, they will teach you regardless. Pink quartz is a good crystal for those who feel troubled getting to love themselves and for those who hardly accept love from others simply because they feel they are not worth of being loved. During cleansing of the stone use the soft waters running in the rivers and last but not least recharge it using moonlight. It is also used as a moon brightener. I had a bad day building up to a bad week, I also had a number or stones lined up for me and I happened to pick one which was rose quartz held on to it, and as the day wore on I realized my mood gradually changed positively and significantly brightened. I actually cannot explain why I was attracted to the stone but one thing is for sure I will always have it in my possession.

Amethyst

Another form of quartz crystal, amethyst is considered by many to be the most beautiful of magical stones. It ranges in color from pale lavender to deep, very dark purple, and may be transparent or opaque. The color is created by the presence of manganese in clear quartz, and the variation in hue is caused by additional amounts of iron. Amethyst frequently occurs in geodes, where it's not uncommon to see amethyst and clear quartz points clustered together. In ancient Greece, amethyst was considered the "stone of sobriety," believed to help reduce the intoxicating effects of wine, and to this day is used in working to break addictions, as well as other unwanted habits and patterns. This is because amethyst has a very high vibration that helps people connect to their spiritual selves and find the balance between healthy indulgences and unhealthy overindulgence. It is a stone of contentment, aiding in meditation and attaining higher states of consciousness and transforming negative energy into positive energy.

While other magical tools call for the creation and accumulation of riches, citrine allows the user to hold on to what they already have so it doesn't slip through their fingers. Citrine's associations with the planet Mercury and the Element of Air, along with its yellow color, makes it an excellent stone for magic relating to concentration, visualization, decision-making and mental clarity in general.

Key words: Clarity, Manifestation, Clearing, Willpower

Zodiac Sign: Gemini

Planet: Mercury

Element: Air

Citrine Stone-Cleansing Ritual

As with all of your magical tools, it's important to keep your crystals and other mineral stones clear of old, unwanted energies.

And of course, be sure your citrine is energetically clear and charged before using it to cleanse your other stones.

Agate

Banded Agate is good at performing metaphysical skills. Agate will aid the stability of the aura, help in balancing emotional, physical and spiritual self and also aid stabilize the aura and also balance the energies. It will give help in self-reflection, grounding and aid communication with the astral entities. It helps taking away bad dreams (nightmares) and instead bring about good brighter dreams. Agate crystal is mainly useful for its protection abilities. The stone will protect against bad dreams, bad weather, stress and energy drains and attacks. It will aid with grounding and balancing. It does not necessarily clear one of undesirable things, but alternatively helps to bring about strength that help you move forward and acceptance. You can have in your possession as you carry on with your life for it influences you to make better decisions. Generally it will sooth emotions, boost self-confidence, bring about calmness and help you dispel your fears.

Agate stimulates intellect, analytical capabilities, precision or and significantly enhance creativity. Agate has medicinal properties.

Agate is used to soothe a stomach that is upset.

It will greatly aid with the respiratory issues.

Agate also can be used to treat issues regarding teeth and gums.

Moonstone

It is also known as the "Traveler's Stone" and has long been a talisman of safe journeys, though these journeys may be inward, soul-searching travels just as much as physical journeys to a far-away location.

In Wiccan magic, moonstone has been used to increase psychic abilities and clairvoyance, relieve stress and foster compassion, and for ritual worship of triple moon-goddesses

Some people keep a moonstone in the glove compartment of their car, and it is said to be good protection against road rage.

Key Words: Clarity, Higher Guidance, Intuition

Zodiac Sign: Cancer

Planet: Moon

Element: Water

Onyx

The gods seems to have gifted us with onyx. At this stage we look at how it can be of assistance to you by improving and leaving a fulfilling life. Onyx is categorized under chalcedony that is also part of the quartz family. It emerged to be a popular stone in Greece. The Greeks had a belief that the onyx stone traced it sourced from the fingernails of a Goddess Venus.

Onyx was a powerful stone known for positive attributes. The stone is a centering and grounding stone. It helps balance you spiritually, emotionally, and mentally. Secondly, the stone is used for strengthening stone and will give you the courage to tackle issues challenging you. Thirdly, it will help diffuse your fears where they seem strongest. Fourth, it takes away negativity. Fifth, it helps rejuvenate or bring back energy when you seem to burn out. Finally, the stone brings happiness and attracts the positive energy to you.

Amber

The name Amber is sourced from the Arabic world. Succinite is derived from the Latin word (succus), which means "juice". The Greeks in the ancient days referred to it to as it (electron).Scientifically Amber is not considered as true stone. It believed to be fossilized resin of trees that are of Oligoncene geological epoch which were in existence in about thirty million years back. They do vary in color from dark brown to pale yellow but over time some specimen of amber have been found that are red in color. Amber is known for attracting and containing small animals and insects of different kinds not forgetting the barks and leaves that get stuck to it when it is still sticky or liquid. At times it's called succinate. Amber is a hard and also very soft as well.

The trees that conveyed the gum found in Baltic amber did grow in present day south-eastern and central Sweden. Then from that point it was brought along by the waters of the rivers to the present day location. Amber is mostly found in northern side and the western side of a town called Kaliningrad (USSR). Other small deposits of amber have been located around the Dominican Republic.

Amber is associated with magic workings. This stone is used as a ward and as an improving stone by Wiccans and the Shamans. Amber is a sensual, magnetic stone and it attracts love. Back in the ancient times amber was used to cleanse the air by burning it. People believed that by gazing to it one would improve their eye sight. The touch and feel of the amber gives such a soothing feel to the nerves. The amber stone with the pale yellow color, are ideal type for healers, they are believed to represent energy be stalled in the sun.

Carnelian

Creative types can benefit from carnelian's ability to move past creative blocks and manifest one's inner vision in the outer world, particularly when one's "inner critic" is the main obstacle. Wiccans have long recognized carnelian's assistance with grounding and aligning with one's spiritual guides, and it makes a good talisman against "psychic attack," or negative thoughts projected by others. It's also good for spellwork related to love and to invigorating a relationship with new sexual passion. As a motivator and activator, it is said to attract prosperity and is good for money-making ventures.

Key words: Grounding, Self-awareness, Vitality, Creativity

Zodiac Sign: Leo

Planet: Sun

Element: Fire

Desert Rose

The Desert Rose has several names, and they are Sand Rose, Gypsum Rose or Selenite Rose. The desert rose is finds its trace in dry regions. Selenite (desert rose) is named after Selene, a Greek goddess said to be of the Moon because it glows like a moon. Usually exchanged between two lovers, it helps bring reconciliation. We have Desert Rose (gypsum rose) metaphysical properties which we find to be mental clarity, also helps increase environment and self awareness, allows you to see and realize the inner truth, aids you to access the angelic guidance, also promotes and triggers the success aspect of a business, it can quickly unblocks the stagnant energy, imparts a deep or bottomless peace, and also helps accessing past lives. They have been traditionally used as talisman protection as we know each one is believed to have a unique guardian spirit.

Jade

Britain to New Zealand, South and Central America all the way to and China, jade was and has been a very important stone, used as a tool and ritual artifacts.

Normally this stone is green and also opaque, although somewhat it may appear to be translucent and at times it comes about in shades of gray, pink and white. Traditionally it has been a symbol of truthfulness, luck, wisdom and tranquility.

On the spiritual and emotional planes, jade will help you learn and realize your authentic self, that inner self that knows deep down the confusion and emotions that are taking place during a particular time. Jade do help in clearing and dealing with past emotions and self-trust that maybe making it difficult to for you to see your ability in the present situations in an objective aspect. It helps you bring out the real you in public and interactions rather than trying to show or present yourself in the way people want to visualize you. The reasons we have discussed above, jade gives calming energy. Jade energy has the ability to create good circumstances in terms of wealth, new opportunities and relationships in the sense that you are putting yourself in the context of the real authentic you.

Jade works greatly in magical workings having the ability to eliminate negativity and protection and giving you access to your own courage and wisdom. By placing on your forehead, it helps you bring about the insight right from your spiritual realms. During your sleep time remember to put it under your pillow, it helps you remember your dreams.

Remember to keep it in your pocket, the green stone helps you keep your immune system in good conditions and helps you get recharged.

Key Words: Transformation, Self-awareness, Manifestation

Zodiac Sign: Pisces

Planet: Neptune

Element: Water

Green Flourite

Green fluorite can be simply be referred to as Flourite. It is teaches us and encourage to embrace and be inter-dimensional. It is used to develop your mind from a single mental reality going forward to the next. Assists in fighting some mental disorder and also helps you gain spiritual awakening. Stabilizes the positive and negative phases of the mind. Injects a lot of energy in you when you are working. And also very focusing indeed. Assists in multiplying the assimilation into the body of Life Force. Flouride strengthens dental issues and bones as well.

Lapis Lazuli

Lapis Lazuli known as lazurite, and can also be shortened to "lapis," this beautiful and striking stone is can found in various shades that is from pale blue to nearly deep indigo blue, most often Lapis has gold inflections and white streaks.

This beautiful stone ancient Egyptians and the Sumerians considered the stone extremely valuable, linking to the celestial through its affiliation with color blue that reflects in sky. Lapis Lazuli is connected with truth, connection and communication, to a higher wisdom. Powerfully and energetically, lapis stone is good at lifting depression and repairing a sense of the inner peace. Such as jade, the stone is associated with or for self-knowledge and it aids you reflect on the way your beliefs and perception get to shape up your choices. It has the ability to stimulate motivation and intuitions, making it much easier to manifest situations that we long for and that are for our own good.

For those people who are knowingly and consciously paying attention to their spiritual journey, Lapis Lazuli helps them maintain the connection and association with the advanced self-being and have access to encouragement from the spiritual level. Lapis also performs on the intellectual heights, fueling our aspiration for knowledge and sense understanding and aiding us to greatly integrate new knowledge, in addition to enhancing memory.

Lapis know as a stone of truth, enable you to effectively communicate honestly to others and yourself as well. Holding a lapis stone in your hand or to the third eye while doing your meditation can help you add and increase your capability to give you the push and confidence to show or express it and to quickly record what is your truth.

Since lapis has the ability and capability to establish clear connection with higher self and can also increase psychic abilities, Wiccans use this stone to fulfill their desired results. Lapis stone is also great influence workings to strengthen friendships and boost or strengthen love relationships, also helps in restoring balance and embracing harmony between our deeper selves and egos. It's considered as an ideal stone to perform spellworks done outdoors especially in the night sky.

Bring with you lapis stone when having communication of all kinds, it might be a meaningful kind of a conversation between friends, or maybe even a big public speaking occasion. This stone can also protect negativity especially that of words or thoughts that might come from other people, and return it back to the source. Key Words: Intuition, Higher Guidance and Communication

We have the:

Zodiac Sign: Libra

Planet: Jupiter

Element: Air

Malachite

Malachite is an opaque stone of deep, rich green with lighter green circular bands that cause many pieces to appear to have an eye. For this reason, the stone was believed in the Middle Ages to ward off negativity and enhance visionary abilities. Malachite is considered a "Stone of Transformation," fostering spiritual growth during times of great change, or inspiring us to make important changes and take emotional risks. Its energy can help you break unwanted patterns that restrict your growth, such as avoiding social situations due to shyness or self-consciousness.

This stone helps build emotional courage and clarity, by helping us learn to recognize and then release old emotional wounds, especially those suffered in childhood. It helps with fear of confrontation, encourages expression of feelings, and promotes healthy, positive relationships and empathy for others.

Malachite is good for protection magic, particularly for people who get easily overwhelmed by the congestion of psychic energy in crowded places. It's good for all travel situations, and particularly aids in fear of flying. It absorbs negative energy, so holding it in the palm of your hand during difficult or frightening situations can bring immediate relief—but be sure to clean and clear it often if you use it for this purpose.

As a green stone, it can be used in any prosperity spell, and is also good in workings for healing emotional wounds. In the workplace, it helps dispel energetic toxins from fluorescent lighting, electrical equipment, and unwanted noise.

Key Words: Self-awareness, Healing, Clarity, Protection

Zodiac Sign: Scorpio

Planet: Venus

Element: Earth

Topaz

Wearing topaz will help you overcome your fears. This is a stone of strength, protection and trust. It helps you get a relieve from depression, fear, anger, tension, insomnia and headaches. Imparts the inner vision and also helps light up direction in the right path. Increases personal abilities. It helps stimulates the intellect side for writers, artists and scientists. It helps creativity and abstract thinking. This stone is believed to have medical properties such as prevention of tuberculosis and strengthens breath.

Tiger's Eye

The energy of tiger's eye is excellent for soothing and resolving emotional turmoil, as it helps you observe emotional patterns from a more distanced, objective standpoint.

Tiger's eye is helpful in this regard for its ability to help you separate fantasy (which arises from emotion) from the reality of the situation.

Additionally, this stone has been used by those with affinities for tigers and other big cats as a prayer stone for their conservation and well-being in the wild as well as in sanctuaries.

Key Words: Clarity, Balance, Vitality

Zodiac Sign: Capricorn and Leo

Planet: Sun

Element: Earth and Fire

Bloodstone

The ancient Mésopotamiens dipped the stones in cold water and applied them to the skin over vital organs for detoxification.

Chapter 12: The Use of Crystals in Spellwork

The introductory list represents just a few of the wide variety of crystals and stones available for use in healing and magic. They have been chosen because of their popularity for use in magic in particular, and their relatively wide availability.

In order to provide opportunities to deepen your acquaintance with some of these stones, the spellwork in the following section draws exclusively from this list. However, as you set out to bring new crystals into your life, always go with your intuition. If a stone not on this list calls to you, then by all means, listen!

Likewise, if you're looking for a particular stone, like jade for example, but don't feel connected to any of the available jade stones in the shop, it may not be time for you to work with jade—or the jade for you may be elsewhere. It's also possible to make substitutions in many of the spells, since it's often the case that a handful of stones are equally suitable to any given purpose. This is especially important to remember if you're on a budget that doesn't have room for a new crystal. Remember, magic should never be a cause for financial stress—in fact, it should be a means of creating more abundance! The next section will introduce you to a few different types of crystal magic, from simple "charge and carry" spells to using crystals in ritual baths, and joining the power of crystals with magically charged candles and herbs.

Because of the mineral and energetic nature of crystals, some of the spellwork requires caution, so be sure to read instructions carefully!

Remember also to spend some time with the stone(s) you plan to work with in your magic. The power of spellwork is much more effective when you have a strong connection to the tools you work with, and this is especially true when working with these natural gifts from the Earth. So approach this work with reverence for the living energies of crystals, and, just as importantly, have fun! Wiccans use stones and crystals to line their sacred circle before they start their ritual. They can be used to honor deities with certain stones that are sacred to certain goddesses and gods. Certain magical tools like pentacles and wands are sometimes decorated with crystals and they are used in all sorts of magical jewelry.

Stones and crystals are used for all sorts of things from manifesting love and wealth to divination to healing. Just like in ancient times, they are still being used for talismans, amulets, other charms for luck, along with protections and scrying. Crystals can add power to your spells whether they are the main focus or as a helper ingredient of the spell.

Amethyst get used a lot as a boost for all sorts of spells. Clear quartz is usually kept on an altar to help sharpen focus, especially if it is a very complex spell. You could also charge a certain crystal for a certain purpose and carry it with you wherever you go such as citrine to attract money or red jasper for courage.

Crystal magic is a great way to work with colors naturally. Crystals aren't dyed like cloth or candles. Vibrant colors will resonate with various aspects of our existence like money, health, and love but according to their own vibrations. Pink that is found in rose quartz, is great for loving vibrations and this makes it great for bringing love to you. Green resonates with abundance and this makes bloodstone and jade great to spells that involve prosperity.

Mineral Stone

There are several different gemstones you can wear during these rituals; which ones you choose depend on what you are trying to accomplish when you are performing the spell. The gemstones give the magic a boost because they can reflect energy as you are performing a spell. If you wear the right stones for the right ritual, you can release a powerful magic without using all the energy in your body. However, it is still a good idea to eat well and be well rested before any ritual because of the amount of energy it takes. You will probably be tired afterward, but that is okay because rituals can take a lot out of even a strong witch. Gemstones will help reduce the amount of energy needed for a ritual so that you may need only a nap rather than to sleep for a full day and a half or more. Some people feel like they are going to go into a coma if they try to perform a ritual that is too complicated for their bodies. Avoid the comatose state; search for stones that are good for certain rituals and wear them shamelessly.

Part 3: Chapter 13: Candle Magic

Candle magic can be related to astrology or elemental magic but also stands alone in some cases. Candle magic has been in existence for many decades, since the inception of Wiccan magic. During the creation of the concept of candle magic, human beings were living at a time where there was immense belief that spirits not only inhabited living things, but were in non-living things as well. Some of the non-living items that the spirits were believed to have inhabited include rocks, dirt, and water elements. Despite their existence, the spirits always required to be appeased so as to manifest themselves. One of the major ways of appeasing them was through fire, which then explains the necessity of a substance such as a candle. Many people believe that the invention of candles occurred soon after the onset of the tradition of appeasing the spirits, since candles are able to burn for a longer time.

Notably, the fire was considered to be both a friend and an enemy of the ancient people, our ancestors. It was a friend, since the people used it to light up the darkness, as a source of warmth in the winter, and even to protect them from wild animals. Also, it was from the discovery of fire that the ancestors finally began to cook, thus doing away with the eating of raw food. On the other hand, fire was also considered to be an enemy, since it was capable of maximum damage, and some people had witnessed their crops, flesh, and even caves and some of the wooden structures which served as their homes burning. The concept of fire was undoubtedly bittersweet, and some people even considered it to be mysterious.

The real connection between fire and magic started when some of the people began to notice that whenever anything was on fire, a smoke emanated which was different depending on what was burned. Some leaves and herbs produced sweet smelling scents, all of which varied from each other, and so did other things such as different animal meats. The people began to believe that with each different type of smoke, a different spirit existed, a factor which increased their curiosity. The smoke always arose, and seemingly went towards the ultimate source of fire (the Sun).

The ancestors also noted that whenever some of the herbs were inhaled, they resulted in out of the ordinary behaviors, such as hallucinations and uncontrolled body reactions. The effects are what is known in the current days as a "high" when people breathe or directly use substances such as weed. The ancient people believed that when such experiences were realized, there was a high chance that the spirits actually inhabited the bodies of the afflicted persons. With such inhabitation, the person had a better chance of interacting with the spirits and carrying out sacred rituals that could appease them. With that knowledge, they began to develop rituals and connected them to the different herbs and plants, and a tradition slowly began to ensue.

As the tradition progressed, generation after generation and throughout the world, the people began to develop alternatives which would ensure that the fire flames lasted much longer than in cases where the people had to rely on the burned leaves only. In ancient Egypt, traditionalists began to melt reeds, and in the process produced torches. The torches could burn for longer, enabling the traditionalists and magicians to cast spells more easily and for longer. Soon afterward, the reed torches evolved to wick candles which were made of rolled papyrus dipped into animal fat. Even though the wick candles were a huge improvement over torches, a disadvantage that ensued was the foul smell of the wicks, which interfered with the natural smell of any herb that was to be used for the rituals. The wick candles also burned unevenly, interfering with the preferred silence and tranquility that was required in a majority of meditation practices. However, a better alternative and development of the candles took a long time, and it was not until the middle ages that beeswax candles were discovered.

The discovery of the process of making beeswax candles marked a revolutionary time in the development of candle magic. Despite the fact that the candles were more expensive, they burned more evenly and had a non-existent to relatively pleasant smell. Due to their expensive nature, the candles were mostly used in special places such as religious gatherings as well as places of magic. Toward the 18th century, more innovations took place, and the discovery of whale oil as a raw material for spermaceti-wax took place. The candles made of the oil were much cleaner and had no scent, which made them very effective for rituals where fire purity without any smoke was required. Whale produces a lot of oil, which made it very easy to get these candles at a cheaper price and more efficiently compared to candles made of beeswax. The candles made of the oil were much more long-lasting, burned brighter, and did not melt easily in hot temperatures. As a result, people and witches who needed candles to perform magic in their households were able to obtain them more easily. With it, spell work became easier and the Wicca tradition became more pronounced and easy.

By the 19th century, the discovery of stearic acid came along, and the candle makers discovered that they were able to harden the wax. Also, aniline dyes, as well as the use of paraffin, made the candles more efficient to create and they could even be made in multiple colors. Many companies had already become established by that time, and mass production of candles was in progress. As more candles became accessible, they increased in popularity in magical practices. Wicca was such tradition, and to date, numerous spells and magical incantations have been developed in accordance with the color of the candles as well as the seasons and significance of the incantation.

Chapter 14: Wonder of Fire: How We Are Connected With Fire

Our earliest human ancestors lived for thousands of years before discovering how to create fire and harness its power—imagine how astounding this discovery must have been! Perhaps because it's the only one of the four Elements that isn't automatically present in any given setting, fire has always had a magical, mystical quality to it. This can be seen in ancient myths, such as the Greek story of Prometheus, who stole fire from the gods and gave it to humankind in order to advance civilization. Similarly, in many Native American traditions, fire is also acquired rather than discovered, usually by animals with more power and ability than humans, who can't get it for themselves. Indeed, fire was seen in many cultures as a mysterious substance that wasn't simply made available to just anyone it had to be acquired, often through the use of quick, clever thinking.

Our connection to fire has never really faded since those early days of our existence. Even today, despite all the innovative technology we use in heating our homes, illuminating our spaces, and powering our electronic devices, we still enjoy the primal quality of fire in the form of indoor hearths, outdoor bonfires, and, of course, candles. Gazing into the flames of a fire can be calming and meditative, a way to transcend ordinary reality and connect with the unseen forces that make the phenomenon of fire possible. The ceremonial use of the element of fire, in the form of candles, is found in most religions, including Judaism and Christianity as well as Buddhism and Hinduism.

But arguably it can be assumed, Wicca (and other forms of Paganism) is where flames of fire really grabs the spot light, as it is used in a variety of ways and forms. Be it a bonfire for an outdoor ritual, a cauldron fire for making a magical brew, or a candle for honoring a deity, they all require fire. Candles are probably the most widely used "instruments" of the Element of Fire, whether they're instigating the transformation of reality, or simply lighting the ritual space.

Chapter 15: Candles in Wiccan Ritual

Like anything else in Wicca, there are traditions that follow as closely as possible the workings of Wicca's modern founders, and there are new, more individualized interpretations developed by later generations of followers. My tip? Take the approach that resonates with you the most. If it feels comfortable and correct to you, it's the right approach for you to take.

Using tea lights in small paper bags weighted with sand or small pebbles is another option, and is particularly handy for outdoor rituals where breezes can make it difficult to keep candles lit.

There are elaborate spells, using many candles along with several other ingredients, and much less involved spells that may only require one simple white tea light.

Preparing Candle for a Ritual

The importance of anointing your candles and preparing them for rituals must not be overlooked. It is important that you charge your candle before you begin any sort of spell casting. In this chapter, we will be looking at how to charge your candle and how to prepare it for ritual use.

If you wish for your candles to work to their full potential when performing candle magick then it is important that you know which specific oils are used in order for you to achieve this. As a beginner, it is sometimes overlooked and frustration is rife when the caster realizes that they skipped an important part of the preparation of the ritual. It is very important to take note of all these things before beginning. Without the knowledge, you cannot perform candle magic to its full effect. Charging your candle gives life to the energy that surrounds it, therefore, making it potent and effective.

When performing candle magic, it is ideal that you use magic oil that serves the same purpose of the chosen candle that you wish to anoint. For example, if you wish to cast a spell for money, then you would need to take a green candle and use a Juniper oil to anoint the candle in order to charge the candle with the intentions that you require. Many southern practitioners in candle magick tend to pray over their candles before anointing them with special oils so that the candle can be rid of any contamination that surrounds it. With the wax of a candle being sticky, it is said that if any intentions - good or bad - before the anointing of a candle have befallen the wax, it could interfere with the spell that you are about to cast. There are many ways that you can use to purify a candle and free it from contamination. Cleansing incantations are popular as well as a simple blessing. As soon as you have done this, you can proceed to anoint your candle with the specific oil that you may need for the spell you desire to cast.

In order to fully cleanse a candle, you must first rid your mind of any negativity and find your center. You will need a calm mind to achieve success and believe fully that the power of the mind can rid the bad from within your candle. When purifying your candle, you will need to hold the candle or cup the candle in your hands and focus intently on cleansing it. As soon as you succumb to the positivity that is flowing within your body and chakras, you will imagine a blue, gold or white light flowing from inside of yourself and making its way into the candle that you grasp, wiping it clean from any contamination, thereby readying it for use.

This practice is often referred to as basic magic visualization that benefits any sort of spiritual or working tradition in regard to the type of candle magick that you wish to perform. To anoint your candle you will need to hold the candle in the hand you don't use as often. For example, if you are right handed then you would use your left hand to hold the candle and vice versa. Then, with your strong hand - whichever that may be - you take the oil that you are going to use, place a drop onto your fingers and proceed to massage the oil onto the top of the candle near the wick before working your way down to the center of the candle. It is important that your candle is completely covered in oil. With your weak hand, pour a drop of the oil into your weak hand and proceed to do the same from the center to the base until the candle is completely glistening in oil.

There is a reason why the anointing of the candle is done in two halves and this is essential. When anointing the first half of the candle, the motion represents taking your petition up towards the heavens before the second motion brings it back down to the material planes so that it can manifest.

With the leftover oil that you will have on your hands, you can use it as an agent to project your will towards solidifying your intentions when performing the spell.

In order to cleanse your candle free from any negativity, you would need to do the reverse from the above. First, you would need to stroke from the middle down and then from the center to the wick. It is important that you remember this. There are many ways that can be chosen when anointing candles. These are too many to name but if you feel that this method is not for you then there are many sources that you can look up on how to properly cleanse your candle. I chose these methods, as they are the most popular ones when it comes to candle purification and are proven to be the most effective.

Many practitioners of candle magick like to inscribe their candles after the initial anointing of the candle. Other practitioners prefer to inscribe their candles with their personal sigil or a special symbol that promotes their intent of using the candle. These can be a certain word related to the ritual. Others prefer to dress their candles in the appropriate attire needed to perform the spell. Candles can be dressed in ribbons, stones or other decorations that are related to the practice in order to strengthen their intent in order to achieve the full power that decorating and inscribing your candles can muster. In order to learn how to properly do these things, you will need to research what your intentions will be in order to match the inscriptions and proper dressing up of your candles.

Below I will list a few examples of what I mean when I talk about symbols and inscriptions. It is important that you know full well what you are going to inscribe before continuing your ritual. Here are a few examples. If money is what you desire then you will need to carve a dollar sign into your candle, which represents financial abundance. If seeking emotional healing or you seek any kind of healing you would need to carve a reiki symbol into your candle in order to project your intentions for the ritual clearly. With this process, you don't have to be an artist to carve beautiful pictures into the wax, just something simple and vaguely recognizable will be fine. You will also need to inscribe these symbols twice on each side of the candle. Once your candle has been inscribed, it should then only be used for that intended purpose. No other purpose should be used once the inscription is carved upon your candle.

Inscribing your candle is a good way of importing your thoughts, energy and intent into the candle whilst focusing on what you desire. Inscribing the candle is preparing it for its intended purpose and once you light the flame you release those intentions. There are many tools that can be used to inscribe the candle. The most preferred method is a small wooden stick or a toothpick that is sharp enough to carve into the wax with a clean cut and smooth precision. Anything with a good sharp point is good for inscriptions but it can also be very dangerous and tricky if not done correctly. The last thing you want to do is to cut yourself when inscribing so please do be very careful when you get to this part of the ritual.

As we move onto the next step of a beginners guide to candle magic, the next chapter will be taking a look at simple spells that are easy for beginners when new to the world of candle magick. It is important that everything I have written you pay heed to, as it will benefit you in the long run. Learning the art of candle magick is a skill and is not right for everyone. If you believe that the art of candle magick is the perfect stepping stone for you before entering into the world of Wicca, then I encourage you to read on. There is so much left to learn.

Chapter 16: Colors and Their Application

In Wicca, color is considered to be a type of energy which is full of vibrations. The color that you are drawn to, and the one that you use during candle rituals, affects the outcome and how you react to different things. The endowment of color with magic has been in existence since time immemorial. The Egyptians were the first to discover the association between color and the different magical elements they support, and it has extended to the current day among the pagans. Notably, each of the colors caries varied vibrational effects which are in relation to the four elements which are the fire, air, water, and earth. Notably, a

Wiccan is supposed to be very conscious about the colors around them, since the colors cement their ideations and knowledge in the subconscious level. When you know what the colors mean, you can be able to respond appropriately to them.

As you know, energy is maximized when it is recognized at even a subconscious level. Therefore, the subconscious works even when the conscious is focused on other things, making the manifestation more prevalent. You cannot live without experiencing color, and everything in this world has color. As you go on with the daily activities in your life, you cannot not be conscious of all the colors around you. The subconscious picks on what the conscious does not, which is why you must strengthen it through color meditations and spells.

When casting candle spells, be very conscious about the colors that you use and ensure you match the candle colors with the intention with which you are casting the spell. Notably, different schools of thought and institutions associate different colors with different meanings. The following is the full Wicca association, and it will help you in the determination of the candle colors to use in your different rituals.

Red Candles

In Wicca, the color red has the following associations:

- The planet Mars

- Day of the week is Tuesday

- Astrological signs are Scorpio and Aries

- The chakra sign is the root

- In numerology, the numbers associated with the red color are 5 and 9.

Red candles are used in the casting of spells which are related to vitality, vigor, and health. The color is considered to be a sign of physical energy that has been bestowed in multiple dimensions such as in sexuality, love, passion, willpower, and ability in athletics. Red is also considered to be a color of danger, and it may be used to arouse lust, anger, and trouble.

The best spells cast with red candles are those in which you require fast action, assertiveness, battle, ambition, strength, passion, and stamina. For instance, you can use the red candles to cast protection, love, self-confidence, and psychic spells. Since the red color is considered to be physical, it is a sign that you can cast spells which will enable you to stay in touch with the power of physical touch. As you know by now, love and romance are some of the major factors and illustrations of physical touch, and using the candles will help you achieve your results. Also, financial prosperity, ambitions, and new realities are created using red candles.

Notably, using red candles when you are casting spells can increase your personal power in a major way. Therefore, you must ensure that you are in a stable state of mind before you attempt to invoke any spell associated with the color. Some Wiccans uses red candles in association with black ones, and the latter is considered to greatly help with the elimination of any negative energy. Your intentions must always remain clean and be in accordance with the major Wicca tenet that asserts that no harm shall befall anyone as a result of your spell. Some people may be tempted to invoke the energies associated with the red candle for their own selfish reasons. As a disclaimer, when you use the red candles for any form of dark magic, you will attract negative extremities such as accidents, bloodshed, increased hatred, and even death. Some shrewd Wiccans use this candle to cause negative occurrences on some people for their own reasons, but the repercussions more or less ripple back to them at some point. Therefore, you are better suited to only use red candles when you want to attract good things into your life and refrain from harming others.

To ensure that the energies are on the maximum when you cast the spells associated with the red candles, ensure that you perform them on Tuesdays and preferably during the waxing moon phase. Other elements that you can add include rubies, pyrites, obsidian, and red tiger eye.

Orange Candles

Therefore, the inferences and energies associated with the color are a combination of those in the red and yellow colors. Normally, yellow is associated with mental agility, while red is considered to be action-oriented as has been described above in depth. With orange, you will gain the benefits of the two, which means that you will be in a better position to benefit from both worlds.

The orange candles are used in spells which are aimed at attracting positivity, success, good fortune, and flourishing in your business and career. The orange color is considered to be very assertive and outgoing, which means that the energies released will be able to encourage fun while discouraging laziness in the same breath. The red element in the orange candles helps with enhancing adaptability, stimulation of sexual inferences, and enabling the natural impulsive vivaciousness. Therefore, the spells which are best cast using an orange candle are those which will promote a happy and lucky appearance. Also, the candles are used in the casting of spells which encourage confidence, increased self-esteem, friendship, and power.

In more positivist traits, the orange candles are a representation of courage, heroism, abundance, business prosperity, and success in matters which pertain to justice and law. You can cast these spells whenever you are attracting positive inferences such as when you are going for a job interview, when making business deals, and generally when you want to attract something that you feel will propel you to the next step and phase in your life. More importantly, there are often times in your life when you may feel that you do not know the direction in which you want your life to follow. In such a case, cast the spell using the orange candles and trust that it will present you with a sign concerning what you should do to achieve whatever it is that you want to. Whenever you do not have any motivation to do things that you know you should be doing, use the orange candle and you can be sure that you will be re-energized to excel in any of your quests. Usually, the lack of motivation can be said to arise from negative attitudes and dissatisfaction. When you use the orange candles, it acts as a sort of cleansing and you can be sure that you are well on your way towards abolishing the negative forces that are holding you back.

Wiccans believe that the color orange is associated with sudden change, which means that any of the people who are bold enough to follow it will always be successful. In the case that you feel that things are not proceeding how you want them to, you can always use the orange candles to be sure that you will be prosperous. You can cast spells either on the eve of major functions such as weddings or in an environment where you feel that you need a favor in an arising event. As has been stated, interviews and business deals are such functions, and with the belief that the orange candle has brought you to favor, you will most definitely be successful.

Keep the following in mind when you are casting spells using the orange candles, and ensure that you work as closely as possible with the associations noted below since that is the only way through which more energy can be harnessed.

- Orange is associated with the sun

- The day of the week is Sunday

- The astrological sign is Leo

- The chakra associated with orange is Sacral

• Numerological connections are 1 and 8

Yellow Candles

Yellow candles are symbolic of increased brainpower, concentration, intellect, as well as creativity and logical learning. Wiccans consider yellow to have an association with the air element as well as the various powers of the mind. Whenever you cast the spells using yellow candles, it helps with increasing logic and intent, which makes it amongst the best choices for people who are engaged in different types of businesses, most especially when there is a need for inspiration and fresh ideas. Whenever you invoke the energy associated with the color yellow, you delve into increased wisdom and you are considered to have control over the benefits of your own mental powers.

The use of yellow candles is very evident in the instances where people are seeking success in temporary and immediate cases such as passing exams. Also, in the case you are facing problems whose source you do not know, the yellow candles can help increase enlightenment. For instance, your company may be doing very poorly all of a sudden and you do not know why. Using the yellow candles can help open the subconscious and help you identify where the problems lie. The fact that yellow results in the defeat of any negative and dark energy that may be over you means that you will have more clarity and in the process can be expected to promote yourself.

The mental clarity obtained is particularly beneficial in the instances where your learning ability is increasing and where your writing and publishing abilities require improvement. In this case, your communication levels are enhanced dramatically and you are more likely to break any mental blockages that can prevent you from using your full potential. Notably, the color yellow is considered to originate from the east. The east is typically associated with a cheerful and vibrant disposition. This positivity is transferred to whatever it is that you may be seeking, and the result is an undoubted success.

You can use yellow candles in the instances where you wish to gain the confidence and approval of other people. The warm energy transferred ensures that the people you are trying to win over develop a very soft spot toward you and the result is a positive interaction. Also, yellow candles can be used in the building of any kind of relationship, be it family or romantic.

In rather extreme and protective practices, you can use the yellow candles to break down any instances of slander, jealousy, and gossip from people who may be wishing you ill. Occasionally, there may be some occurrences which threaten your relationship with other people. When people gossip and spread rumors about you, it can influence what the recipients of the information think about you. You can use the yellow candles to cast spells which will result in the revelation of the truth, and this means that the words of the people who are against you will fall apart. In such a case, the energy is protective, and it ensures that no single person who is against you will prosper under any condition.

The yellow color is associated with:

• The planet Mercury

• Wednesday day of the week

• The solar plexus Chakra

• Gemini and Virgo astrological signs

• Numerological figures 1 and 12

Green Candles

Green is a color associated with new beginnings, fertility, nature, renewal, and rejuvenation according to Wicca. Usually, financial prosperity, good health, and healing are associated with green, which makes it the best when you are casting spells that are related to such inferences. Lighting green candles is best done in cases when you wish to cast spells which are related to the aspects mentioned or when you want to meditate and focus on different types of prosperity. Usually, Wiccans believe that the green color triggers all forms of growth and success, ranging from the money in your wallet to your finances and crops. Therefore, the best spells are those that are inclined toward the building of wealth as well as self-love and fulfillment.

Whenever you cast spells through the invoking of green candles, you should have the intention of invoking a new beginning into your life that is full of greatness and fulfillment. Note that green is different from red in the sense that red invokes energies related to passion and romance, while green is more permanent and may be a representation of solid marriage and faithfulness. Whenever you use the green candles, you can be sure that you will have more permanent and long-lasting relationships and that the invoked heart chakra will work by ensuring that all your romantic conquests are meaningful. Evidently, this is a sign that it is attracting luck.

The common associations of the green candles are:

- It relates to the planet Venus

- The best day to invoke the energies and the spirits is on Friday

- It relates to the heart chakra

- The astronomical relations are Taurus and Libra

- The numerological associations are 2, 3, and 7

Blue Candles

Blue is a very subtle color that is related to the spiritual well-being of a person, as well as tranquility, serenity, calm, healing, and rest. The subtle meaning and use of the blue color extends beyond pagan and Wicca rituals, and it is used all over the world by other people, too. When you visit many hospitals, they are usually painted blue. Medics assert that the blue color gives the patients some peace of mind which ensures that they have a better chance of improving and consequently getting sleep and rest in their rather unfortunate circumstances. Also, many bedrooms have light blue colors to ensure that the inhabitants get to relax their minds so that they can have better sleep.

You are supposed to use blue candles whenever you are not in the right state of mind and when you have increased feelings of indecisiveness and anxiety. Often, the first thing that you are supposed to do is meditate and visualize the blue color of the candle so that you can relax and ensure that your brain is in the best position to cast any spells as well as perform any of the Wicca rituals. Meditation is also important in the case that you feel as though you do not have sufficient faith and hope, a factor which may result in the sabotaging of the spell altogether.

Notably, the uses of the blue candle cannot be exhausted. Every fear and lack of courage can be solved using the blue candle. From the fear of flying, relationships, or even performing any activity, the burning of the blue candle ensures that you get the courage that you crave and ensure that you go through activities with the utmost ease. Some Wiccans have even used blue candles to break some addictions that have been stubborn, including drug and alcohol abuse. You can cast peace spells using candles, and the energy ensures that peace replaces any element of anger, hate, and violence in a particular place. You should note that the blue color is associated with the element of water and the west direction. Typically, water is a sign of tranquility, which explains why the color is said to be calming, too. Above all of this, the blue energy is protective, and it will in most cases ensure that your mental well-being is taken care of. As you know by now, when you are mentally stable, you are able to deal with anything that comes your way.

The elemental associations of the color blue are:

- The planet Jupiter

- Thursday day of the week

- The Throat Chakra

- Sagittarius and Pisces astrological signs

- 4 and 6 in numerology

Purple Candles

Purple is considered to be a color representing the third eye, which is a spiritual illustration of a higher level of awakening and being conscious of things that are beyond the typical knowledge and undertakings. Whenever you light a purple candle, it is an illustration that you are seeking a very high level of consciousness and hidden knowledge. Whenever you cast any spells or conduct rituals using purple candles, it is a sign that you are seeking something that is much higher than what the typical people can perceive as well as an aura that is much higher than what people typically believe in and relate to. When you cast spells and conduct rituals using purple candles, you are bound to achieve a level of awareness that you did not think was possible. You should seek guidance in the areas of your life that you are finding hard to connect with, and through the purple energy you will be able to get answers that you seek.

Notably, the protective nature of the purple candle ensures that you are able to cancel out any negative inferences that may come your way. Some of the negative inferences may include the negative extremities of Karma, a condition which is considered to be jinxed, and bad spells that may be cast towards you by other people. The protection is particularly effective against black magic, and once you cast the spell you can be sure that any negativity in your life shall be permanently removed.

Purple is associated with:

• The planet Jupiter

• Thursday day of the week

• The 3rd eye in chakra

• Sagittarius and Pisces astrological signs

• 7 and 8 in numerology

White Candles

White is considered to be a color of purity, and it is associated with cleansing, protection, blessings, healing, peace, chastity, and many other positive connotations. Usually, the white candles are considered to be an illustration of the highest form of spirituality as well as consciousness level. Notably, all colors are derived from the pure white light which makes it subject to the highest form of vibration and energy. Usually, all the energy derived from the vibration is positive and therefore there is an elimination of any negativity and retrogressive energies.

You are supposed to use white candles when you are casting protective spells, consecration, and any rituals which are considered to be cleansing. Since the color white is untouchable, you can use it in the healing of emotions, children, pets, any acts of violence such as rape, and attracting protection against any enemies that may want to harm you. In the case the white candle is used in black magic, it is known to potentially attract weaknesses, fear, and may destroy the sex drive of the afflicted person.

Some of the associations of white candles include:

- The waxing moon

- Monday day of the week

- The crown chakra

- The Cancer astrological sign

- 1, 2, 5, 7, and 9 numerological figures

Black Candles

Black candles are often associated with negative energy, and most people think that they cannot be used in the casting of positive spells. That is far from the truth. Black candles are known to be imperative in the casting of positive spells such as protection and repelling any black and negative energy that may have been cast against you. Whenever you are feeling confused, are ridden with bad habits, and need something to help with healing, black candles are the best bet toward breaking the negative extremities that may inhibit you. Sometimes, you may not even be aware of these forces. Through the black candles, all negativities toward you, whether known or unknown, shall be banished in entirety.

The black color is associated with the opening of the subconscious mind. In casting spells and generally protecting oneself, you need to take care of the subconscious mind since it generally possesses more energy and you will be able to achieve more when it is activated. Black absorbs energy and lights, and it is the same case where there are negative forces that are working against you. Through neutralization and ensuring that the energies no longer have force against you, the end result is that you are a better person and you will be able to live a more fulfilled life in the long run. Some of the spells which are best carried out using the black candles are healing and wellness rituals, banishing of bad energy, and the exorcism of "evil spirits." You can also use the candles to foster deep meditation and open up the subconscious mind to levels which you did not think were possible. In so doing, the candles help in the achievement of what is known as a new beginning.

Some of the associations of black candles include:

- The planet Saturn

- Saturday day of the week

- The Root Chakra

- Capricorn and Aquarius astrological signs

- 8 and 13 numerological figures

Silver Candles

Silver candles are used in the destruction and dissolving of all negativity that may be upon a person and consequently ensures that they become victorious. Usually, the silver candle is a representation of good things taking over what was evil. When you cast spells using this candle, you can be sure that each and every thing that you put your mind to will be victorious and that no evil forces can stop you.

The strength of the silver candles is usually at the maximum when there is a full moon. Strive to cast any of the spells during this time, and you will realize the most success.

The elemental correspondences of the silver candles are:

• Related to the water element

• West direction

• Monday day of the week

• The Moon

- Midwinter and Samhain sabbats

- Lunar deities

Chapter 17: How to Choose Candles

Votive candles are similarly shaped but generally around twice the size of tea lights. Some Witches embrace the "mess," making it part of the magical process and even divining messages from the Spirit world in the shapes of the melted wax.

However, a candle of this shape made of clean-melting wax and burned in a still space may leave very little dripped wax behind.

Beyond size and shape, there are other considerations involved in choosing candles for magical use the question of scent is a big one.

The length of burning time is also something to think about, particularly for candles used in spells that are meant to be left to burn down on their own.

Even the most conscientious of people can accidentally cause a terrible fire, so it's always better to be safe than sorry!

This means making clear distinctions between candles you use simply for atmosphere, and candles you use for magic. Don't work a spell using a candle that has already been lit for another purpose, even if it was only for atmosphere.

You can even direct that enhancement to help in a particular area of your life by choosing a specific color and location in your home, as we will see later on. Candle magic does only consist of the lighting of a candle and wishing for what you want most in life. Think back to when you were a child and you were sitting in front of a great birthday cake with tiny little candles flickering upon the icing waiting for you to blow them out. Has it ever occurred to you why we are always told to make a wish when we blow out the flame? The motion of closing our eyes as tightly as possible and then taking a great big breath before releasing it to blow out the flame is significant. In candle magic, the ritual is no different. The only difference is that when candle magic is used the flame is not extinguished and practitioners don't close their eyes. What I am trying to tell you is that in order for your spell to work, you must envision what you truly desire but above all things, you must truly believe that your spell will work.

Candle magic relies on the power of the mind. If you are doubtful that your spell will work then, in retrospect, your spell will not. Candle magic is all about the power of the mind. In order for you to gain success with your magic, you need to believe that it will work. You have to put all your faith into the spell that you are casting or else fear the disappointment when it does not work. So far in this book, I have covered many important factors about the art of candle magic. In this chapter, we will look at tips for performing your spells whilst using candle magic.

I have already mentioned that the power of the mind is essential when using candle magic and I would argue that this tip is the number one rule in order for you to gain success. It is important that you believe in your magic. You need to become at one with the spell and the candle that you have dressed and prepared for your ritual and now you must feed into the flame your desire for whatever it is you wish.

Sometimes when using candle magic, there is a long period of time where you are waiting anxiously to see if your spell has worked and are paying attention to your daily life waiting to see if it has had any effect. This can be very draining on the mind but there are ways to avoid feeling anxious and disappointed.

Once you have performed your magic, there is then the break of going back to your daily chores. Many practitioners of magic, professional or novice, sometimes feel impatient when it comes to seeing how their magic will affect the world around them. Sometimes magic takes longer to work, depending on what you wished for, and while sometimes the magic can take a long time to work, other spells could work instantly. In candle magic, it is important that you set a certain amount of time for your spell to work. It is important that you monitor the amount of time it took for your spell to work. For example, you could set a time limit of a week, two weeks or even a month but once that time limit is up and there has been no change, then you perform your spell all over again before setting an allocated time for waiting.

Sometimes in candle magic, the spell caster can get disheartened when they find that no change has affected their lives. This is sometimes due to what you wish for. If you come to find that after the second attempt of magic does not work, then there is a chance that your desire is simply not in the cards for you at this time of your life but it might be in the cards for you later on in your life. When using candle magic, it is important that you don't give up on your magic. Candle magic requires patience and understanding. There is always another time to try again. Never give up.

Another important tip that you must know is for when your magic does work. It is very important to thank the gods. When you see that your magic has worked, you will feel a great uplifting sensation of accomplishment. This feeling is good for when wanting to cast another spell. All the positivity that you feel from the success of your first spell you can project into other spells in order to feed them positive vibes.

Another tip that is good to have before performing your candle spell is something called a magical sweep. This entails envisioning what you want and the tools that will help your magic to work. Collecting ingredients in order to help strengthen your magic is important, as with all the necessary bits and pieces that you are collecting, you are enhancing your magic. In order to help strengthen your magic, many practitioners start by writing down a simple paragraph of what they desire. With this practice, they then simply shorten down the paragraph until it is a sentence and then one word.

That one word must describe the thing you want most and it must be relevant. In candle magic, energy is a great part of the practice. Knowing the energy that you are working with is essential. Just as with the oils and the many relevant candles, knowing what energy you need to work with is no different. For example, if you were seeking love and compassion then the energy source that you would need to call upon would be Kuan-yin. Knowing your gods and the energy they bring forth is a good way to understand how candle magic works. In later chapters, we will look at the different gods and their relevance to candle magic.

Crystals are also a good way of enhancing your magic. This chapter concludes the relevant tips for enhancing your magic when casting your spells. In the next chapter, we will look at the different energies and what relevance they have with candle magic.

Chapter 18: Consecrating Your Candles

Like any other tool used in magic, candles are far, far more effective if they are specifically prepared for use in ritual. The physical thought energy of your intention will find a clearer path to the spiritual realm if the physical candle itself is primed for magic. Terms for the process, and the number of steps in the process, will depend on the tradition of each practitioner, but the objective is essentially the same.

This could be energy left from a prior owner or even someone who gave you the candle as a gift. What's required here is a vibrational clearing away of any energetic imprints that may obstruct the path of the intention as it makes its way into the spiritual realm.

There are many, many methods of clearing objects used in magic, but not all are appropriate for every kind of object. For example, athames can be cleansed by passing the blade through a candle flame, but this obviously isn't ideal for a candle itself, as you're just going to start melting the wax before the spell.

Candles that feel particularly in need of a stronger cleansing can be held under running water (except for the wick), or rubbed gently with a small amount of rubbing alcohol on a soft cloth.

Do what feels right for you which may vary from occasion to occasion but it's advisable to refresh any objects that have been sitting around for a long time collecting dust, or stored among non-magical items, before using them.

If you're the type to stock up and save, wrapping your candles in tissue paper or cloth and keeping them with other magical tools is a nice way to keep them ready to use. You'll learn to sense whether a candle or other tool you've had on hand for a while could use some energetic sprucing up.

Charging

This step is a way to communicate to the spiritual plane that you are working to change some aspect of reality. Not every candle is necessarily going to be used directly in a spell, however, so the way you charge your candles may depend on how you plan to use them.

These approaches are particularly good for atmospheric candles, and also work for altar candles representing deities or Elements.

Hold the candle in your hands and focus on your goal.

Words are a powerful tool of magic and most Witches consider them essential to the act of consecration. Chants, prayers, affirmations, etc. spoken aloud (or silently, if need be) help you focus your energy on the task at hand and communicate your specific intentions directly to the unseen world. You can use one of the following examples, or come up with your own verbalization of the transformation you're initiating.

For example, you might say:

"I charge this candle

through the Universal power

to bring good luck and health

to all in my household.

So let it be."

Whatever words you choose, you should be comfortable with what you're saying.

Anointing

For some, this is not a third step, but is done at the time of consecrating with words as described above. Others rarely, if ever, use oil.

For example, lavender oil is good for working to remove anxiety, and patchouli is associated with prosperity.

Both single oils and pre-made magical blends can be found in metaphysical/occult shops as well as online, and recipes for homemade blends are widely available. If you're lacking access to essential oils or if they're out of your budget range (or if you're simply into a DIY style of magic), you can also fashion your own anointing oils by adding dried herbs to olive or sweet almond oil.

A small spell candle, for example, might only need one drop.

For attracting positive things, you can start at the top of the candle and rub the oil in a downward motion toward the middle.

You may wish to try both methods to see what feels right to you. Consecrating and anointing your candle as close to the spellwork as possible is ideal, but caution is extremely important when working with oil, especially if you're anointing during the spell itself. Too much oil can cause the flame to burn too high, and/or overpower the wick, and there's risk of burning your fingers if you're not careful.

To really be on the safe side, you can use a cloth (consecrated for the purpose, of course!) as an intermediary between your fingers and the candle.

Part 4: Chapter 19: Candle Magic Spells

Candles are important when it comes to Wiccan spells. When extinguishing a candle, you don't want to blow it out unless you have to. Many people do often say candle magic certainly is the oldest kind of magic recorded in the history of human beings. It does not matter if this is true; it is true that fire has always been sacred to the pagan ancestors what supplicated and honored their gods with candles, torches, flaming wheels, and balefires. Since the fire was the only source of light other than the moon and sun until the early 1900s, it is easy to see why fire is a symbol of power through history. The reverence for fire has continued for a long time even after modern lighting caught on. Most religions today still use candles, whether in formal services or when lighting a votive for certain intentions.

Candle magic is the easiest way to cast spells, and because of this, it does not take many ceremonial or ritual tools. Basically, anybody who has a candle could cast a spell. Remember back to when you had a birthday party. You always made a wish before you blew out your candles. This is the same idea behind candle magic. Rather than just "hoping" that your wish comes true, you will be declaring your intent. Nobody remembers where that tradition originated from, and they will not be able to remember who came up with the notion of using candles for magic.

There is something very pleasant about the flicker of a candle flame. It makes us feel peaceful and at ease when we look into that living, dancing, flickering light. Lighting a candle is the easiest way to start shifting out of this reality and connecting with all the unseen energies that are around us all the time. It does not matter if you want to cast a spell or not. Candle spells are straightforward, elegant, and simple. They can help you strengthen and build your "magic muscles" or your ability to direct and focus your energy into your intentions. It is the powerful thoughts that are underneath both the simple and most complex types of magic.

Magic is an art form that sends a specific thought out into the spiritual plane where it gets manifested and then returned back to you on the Earthly plane. For people who are just beginning, candles are great messengers. The request that you are making is being sent through the flame. This request is called an intention. The flame is the medium here. While the candle burns, it will leave the material plane and goes into the ethereal one. It carries your intention with it. If you are a beginner to magic, this example can help you visualize the process.

Think about the birthday candle again for a moment. That ritual is based on three principles:

- Figure out a goal.

- Imagine the end result you want.

- Focus your will or intent to make the result happen.

Charge Your Candles

Before you begin any spell, you always need to take time to charge the items you will use.

Chapter 20: Moonlight Attraction

- Place the vial in front of candle so that it stands between the candle and the window.

- Take a few moments to call up the feelings of well-being, excitement, and companionship. Hold this feeling as you get ready to light the candle. As you light it, say these (or your own) words:

"By this moon's light, let love shine bright."

Chapter 21: Finding Your Ideal Partner Spell

Many of us search for our soulmates over our lifetime. Remember that many people have different ideas about who a soulmate really is. For example, some people believe we only have one soulmate. Another viewpoint is that there are many others out there who we are attracted to on a deep level, those who will encourage us to grow and find deeper love in our lives.

For those who are ready to move beyond casual dating and want assistance in manifesting a solid, healthy relationship.

For example, if you know that sharp intelligence and ability with language are key, you might choose a yellow candle. If no colors or qualities jump out at you as being at the top of the list, then feel free to use a white candle.

Moon phase: Waxing

Ideal day: Friday

You will need:

• 1 small candle (white, or color of your choice)

• 1 gold or silver ribbon, long enough to wrap around your palm at least twice

Chapter 22: Money Spell

Money spells are also known as prosperity spells. Notably, the needs of each individual person are different, and that means that no two spells give the same results. Also, there is a need to demystify the fact that whenever you make the money spells, it does not mean that you no longer have to work or put effort in, since money cannot magically appear into your life from nowhere. Rather, prosperity spells have the major aim of acting as a guide, and helping open your eyes towards the immense opportunities which result in your breakthrough. Whenever the mindset of a person is changed, so is their overall functionality.

Whenever you cast the money and prosperity spells, the major change that occurs is on the subconscious mind of a person. Normally, the subconscious is a powerful yet under-valued part of the brain which connects with the energies, and when it is tuned right you can be able to achieve anything and everything. You are better suited to cast the spell on either a Thursday or Sunday. If there is a moon visible, cast the spell during the waxing phase.

One of the candle rituals of casting the money and prosperity spells is the involvement of 16 candles. The colors of the candles are very specific, and you need 6 green, 9 white, and one gold. You also need some pine oil to consecrate and dress the candles, as well as a little salt. As is obvious, the first step is the covering of all the candles with the oil. When you are done, arrange the candles in the following order:

1) The gold candle at the middle

2) Green candles around the gold candle

3) White candles on the outermost section around the green candles

Instructions:

- Light all the candles one by one, taking time to give each and every one of the candles a little attention. You must light the candles in a clockwise direction as you chant:

Repeat this phrase for a number of times, and then meditate on all of your money needs. Once you are done, you must blow out the candles in the reverse direction you lit them in. Note that you should never blow out the candles entirely, but rather kill the flame using your fingers or allow them to burn out.

Chapter 23: Healing Spell

This spell is very easy, and you can conduct it on yourself whenever you feel sick and under the weather. To conduct this type of healing, you need to be relatively strong, which means that the illness should not be too inhibiting and limiting. For any spell to be successful, you must begin and end it without fail. Therefore, you just be certain that you will be able to get through the casting of the spell in your condition. This is often the strategy used when the healing is being conducted by one or a group of Wiccan ritualists to instigate the healing of another. The aim of this spell is to facilitate the healing of any illness that may be in your body, and the consequent casting of a protective spell to ensure that the sickness does not find its way back into the body.

To successfully conduct this spell, you need 13 eggs, salt, and candles in accordance to the disease that you are healing. The following are the colors of candles and the ailments that are associated with healing:

• White candles are in most cases universal, and are the most preferred when you do not know exactly what a person is suffering from.

• The black candles are considered to be very impartial when the ailing person is proven to be suffering from infections and cancers.

• The orange and yellow candles help in the healing of any ailment which has fatigue as a symptom.

- Brown candles are considered to be related to the earth, and they help with the dealing of ailments which are mostly as a result of stress.

- Purple candles are used to increase the willpower of the sick person to survive. This is mostly the case when such people behave in a way which seemingly indicates that they have lost hope in life.

Once you have assembled these materials, make a wide circle using the salt and have the sick person lay at the center. If you perform this ritual during a full moon, ensure that the person is laid outside, as that is where the healing energy is at its strongest. In the case that there is no moon, continue with the spell as is.

Instructions:

- First, you should light the candles that you have decided are the best for the healing practice and place them either at the altar or around the ill person if you have several. Observe safety when you are doing this, as you may knock over the candles and cause a serious accident. Tell the sick person to be at ease, and to let go of all the mental blockages and inhibitions that they may have at that particular time. It is very imperative for the sick person to have a positive energy regardless of how sick they are, because if they do not the energies will collide and it may not be successful.

- Rub the eggs, one after the other, as the person is still lying down with their eyes closed. It would be ideal for the sick person to be naked for the most part, and you can cover their privates with a small cloth. The eggs are supposed to be rubbed over the body, hence the need for nudity. If the person is very weak, encourage them to meditate on their healing as much as they can and try to focus on what is happening. If the person has some level of strength; they can chant the following affirmations either out loud or within themselves:

Notably, this spell is not meant to be cast on one day and occasion only. Rather, you can conduct it over and over again until the sick person fully recovers. Ensure that you thank the gods after every spell, since gratitude is one of the functions that results in the obtaining of positive energy.

Chapter 24: Employment Spell

Job hunting can be stressful and frustrating, especially if you don't have a lot of experience. These spells can boost your power during this time of reckoning with the unknown! This simple spell is perfect for those who lean towards getting anxious about or if or not a spell is responding positively, for you have several chances to repeat the spell though you should not need a lot of them!

Begin this spell on a Sunday, of which Sunday is the day in a calendar associated with matters to do with work and also career matters.

Moon phase: Should be any

Ideal day: Should be Sundays

You will require:

• 1 yellow or gold candle

Instructions:

Repeat the spell each Sunday until the candle has burned down completely, or until you find a job—whichever comes first.

Chapter 25: Good Luck Spell

This is a good spell for beginners, or for anyone wanting a little practice in focusing on an intention with rather low stakes, but fun results. You'll be delightfully surprised by the ways this spell can come back to you. The trick is to be general in your request—don't ask for good news regarding matters you're overly anxious about at the moment, or any kind of specific outcome, since this can really muddy the energy you're sending out.

- Finally, say Open my eyes and my ears to good fortune, and then light the white candle.

- Carve one to three words that represent the question into the candle, starting at the bottom and working up to the tip.

- Light the candle, and burn the strip of paper.

Allow the candle to burn down.

Chapter 26: Courage Spell

This spell is known to bring courage in the toughest situations, such as war. It will give you a protective shield which will help you establish internal courage so you can carry on with the task at hand. It doesn't matter what you need courage for, this spell will help you with anything from meeting your significant other's family for the first time to public speaking.

- Place the crystal or other object in the center of the square.

However, because thought is energy, it's definitely possible to be undermined by the negative thoughts of others—particularly those who may be resentful or envious of us for whatever reason. Moon phase: Waning.

Ideal day: Tuesday or Saturday

You will need:

• 1 black candle

• 5 garlic cloves

• 1 teaspoon honey

Instructions:

- Arrange the garlic cloves around the black candle in the shape of a five-pointed star.

- Light the candle, and eat the honey.

When the spell is done, bury the garlic cloves outside.

Chapter 27: Banishing Depression Spell

We all find ourselves with a case of the blues now and then.

• 1 piece quartz crystal (or other white stone)

• Small black cloth

Instructions:

- "I release and banish all negativity from my being."

- Visualize your entire body flooded with, and surrounded by, white light.

- Use the black cloth to pick up the black stone so that you avoid touching it with your skin. Keep the quartz crystal (or white stone) in your pocket or in a pouch that you keep near you at all times. You may also want to keep it near your bed while you sleep.

Just be sure to use all three of them until they are completely gone.

Conclusion

You now have a basic overview of the purpose of the Wiccan altar and the tools of ritual and spellwork, as well as some common-sense advice for finding, acquiring, and preparing these items for use in your own Wiccan practice. Although on one level, this guide may seem to cover rather mundane topics, the belief in Wicca is that the divine is in all things because the Goddess and God created everything in our world. We learn that there is equally as much divinity be stored in each and every one of us as much as there is in the seas and ocean, and given that as much as there is power stowed in the branch of the tree just as in the pillar of a temple. Comparably, when we commit a physical object such as a chalice or a wand to tracking down spiritual connection, it results to such.

As you gradually build your own collection of spiritual items, pay attention to how your personal energy feels when interacting with these tools. With time and practice, you will likely find that they become more and more infused with your personal power, and that the quality of focus and energy in ritual and spellwork rises over time. You will find yourself growing and changing in miraculous ways when you work with the daylight of the God and the moonlight of the Goddess. If you approach your new altar and your new tools with joy and reverence, and are willing to learn and practice, you will learn about your own spiritual power, heal, help others, and help yourself traverse the sometimes-rocky road that's known as life.

Finally, although we've just spent a good deal of energy itemizing the rather long list of tools and other items generally considered to be necessary for Wiccan practice, it's important to stress that nothing at all is required for connecting with the Goddess and God beyond your mind, your heart, and your spirit.

Remember that there is no wrong way to practice your faith. Just because one person tells you that you need a particular tool, doesn't make it so. Wicca is all about following your own path, and if you've put off and put off acquiring, say, a robe, it might be your intuition telling you that a particular item is not for you. Perhaps over time your stance will change—that decision is yours to make, though. On that note, it's time to conclude this book. I hope that this guide has provided you with a solid understanding of the Wicca altar, as well as introducing you to the main tools and supplies of our religion.

It has been an absolute pleasure writing this book, and I hope you have enjoyed reading it.

Thank you one more time for reading.